THE
LAST
WAR

THE LAST WAR

THE FAILURE OF THE PEACE PROCESS AND THE COMING BATTLE FOR JERUSALEM

DAVID ALLEN LEWIS
WITH JIM FLETCHER

New Leaf Press

First printing: March 2001

ISBN: 0-89221-503-8
Library of Congress Catalog Number: 00-110219

Printed in the United States of America

Please visit our website for other great titles:
www.newleafpress.net

For information regarding publicity for author
interviews contact Dianna Fletcher at (870) 438-5288.

Dedicated

to

ALAN SHAWN FEINSTEIN
PATRON OF THE POOR AND NEEDY

In Appreciation

I wish to express my deepest appreciation to October Curtis, Chuck Heidle, Mary Hitchcock, Rita Ingebritson, Ramona Lewis, Jenny and Jeremiah Mustered, Connie Ramsey, Jennifer Strohm, and Miriam and Shawn Wamsley for all of their assistance in bringing this book project to a conclusion.

Also, thanks to all of those who helped us in Israel, Moshe Auman, David Bar-Illan, Thomas and Becky Brimmer, Ron Cantrell, Jim Fletcher, Ra'anan Gissim, Michael Glatzner, Neil and Sandy Howell, Harry Hurvitz, Yakov Kirschen, Rani Levy, Yehuda Levy, Avi Lipkin, Johann Luckhoff, Ron Nachman, Armando Nuñez, Ehud Olmert, Yehuda Oppenheim, Avigdor Rosenberg, Gershon Salomon, Ariel Sharon, Eleanora Shifrin, Ed Smelser, Rose Stott, Clarence Wagner, and Bob Zassler.

And finally, to my gracious publisher, Tim Dudley, who is a great inspiration to us all.

Contents

PREFACE

A light rain fell as I watched the drops splashing on the ancient paving stones of the Temple Mount, Jerusalem's holiest site for Jews. It is also revered by the Muslims, to whom the area is known as the Haram el al Sharif, the Most Noble Sanctuary. Behind me stood the golden Dome of the Rock, sometimes mistakenly called the Mosque of Omar. As Palestinians streamed past me into the Al-Aqsa Mosque, I thought of the Jewish worshippers I had been standing with only moments before, just beyond and below a retaining wall — the Western Wall.

On my 64th trip to Israel, I pondered the great things that had happened here on the Temple Mount. Here, the Patriarch Abraham had come, prepared to offer up his son Isaac as a sacrifice. King David had purchased this mountain, and here his son, King Solomon, erected the most magnificent temple of all time. I realized that even today it is the most desired piece of land on earth — the Jews, the Vatican, the Muslims, all claiming right of ownership. One would think that this should be a peaceful spot, but not so! I sensed that I was in the eye of the storm. Somehow the whole world seems to have a gut feeling that here the last war could break out at any moment.

On this particular journey to the Holy Land, I had come for the express purpose of finding out why the peace process seemed to be bogged down. Why couldn't these two brothers, Isaac and Ishmael, Jews and Arabs, solve their deepest problems? Is this just a family feud, or as some ponder, does what happen here really have an impact on world peace? Trouble, trouble, trouble! Not only the Middle East is bogged down in a quagmire of unrest, but the whole world is beset with wars and rumors of wars. Dire circumstances command our attention today. On one hand, terrorists wreak havoc; on the other, regular armies clash on the field of battle.

If ever in the history of mankind we could hear the hoofbeats of the red horseman of the Apocalypse, it is today as he rides roughshod across the earth, and following him is the ominous black horse of famine. In this troubled world, 30 thousand children die daily from starvation. Even here in our own nation we are plagued with acts of terrorism, both domestic and imported. Madness haunts our streets as we gun down each other in drive-by shootings, school massacres, and murders from McDonald's to the post office. The world is full of problems . . . and promise.

Technological advances have opened tantalizing vistas, and we seem to glimpse good things on the horizon of tomorrow. Like an unseen hand, however, it's the problems that pull at us, always keeping real progress just out of reach. While coping with all of our domestic problems, it's hard to realize that the world's most vexing trouble today blows across the sands of the Middle East. I think that it is imperative that we begin now to educate ourselves and force our understanding to reach across the cultural and geographical divides, not only for the accumulation of knowledge, but to insure our own survival.

For more than 40 years, I have immersed myself in the intricacies of relations between Jews and Arabs in the "Holy Land." I sadly conclude that, except for brief respites, it has been anything but holy. In 1982, I found myself in Lebanon during the war, as a journalist seeking answers. The bombs were falling on Beruit and artillery fired all around us. Along the front lines in the Lebanon War, I saw for myself the bloodlust in men's hearts. In that same year, I set my hands on the Rubik's cube of peace, and for a while it seemed that meetings between Israeli and Palestinian leaders, convened in the town of Ramalla, might bear fruit; but, alas, this was not to be. The fighting continues until today, when we find Israel and the Palestinians engaged in Intifada II. Our efforts simply failed like those of other, more well-known seekers of peace.

How important is all of this to my American friends? Should we care about the feudings of a cantankerous family? Why should we waste valuable time and resources on resolving tensions in a far-off corner of the world? "They" have always fought and always will fight. There have been major wars: in 1948, the War of Independence; 1956, the Suez/Sinai War; 1967, the Six Days War; 1973, the Yom Kippur War; 1982, the Lebanon/Peace for Galilee War; 1987, Intifada I; and currently, Intifida II, or the Al-Aqsa War. Correspondents, generals, national leaders, historians, and researchers voice a general agreement that a war in the Middle East could spark a global conflict.

In this book, I hope to show you two things: the basic information about the conflict you perhaps have wondered about from time to time, as Walter Cronkite, Peter Jennings, and others have reported through the decades, and, more importantly, why the issue should be much higher on your list of things to think about.

In the pages that follow, I will do my level best to blend quite a lot of basic information with a dash of insight. I invite you to study and pay attention. Think of this as a handbook of historical, religious, and political realities in the Middle East — a primer of sorts.

Come with me and we will travel to Israel and her neighbors: Jordan, Iraq, Saudi Arabia, Syria, Egypt, and Lebanon. Find out what it all means.

Come stand with me in the rain.

INTRODUCTION

In his 1869 travelogue *Innocents Abroad*, Mark Twain gave a detailed account of his visit to the Holy Land. In describing the arid, desolate scenes, the alter-ego of Tom Sawyer and Huck Finn remarked on the biblical pronouncements that the land would one day flower again.

> Palestine is desolate and unlovely. And why should it be otherwise? Can the curse of the Deity beautify a land? Palestine is no more of this workaday world. It is sacred to poetry and tradition – it is dreamland.

Twain once thought that a plan for the Middle East belonged in never-never land. It seemed so far-fetched. The desert, all its lizards and sparse trees and rocks, would remain a haunt of jackals.

But the Jews came back. Were the old prophets right after all? To be fair, there was an Arab population in the land as well. This is one of the sources of conflict to this day.

Today, in contrast to Twain's colorful description, the land is bursting with color and lush vegetation. It is also witness to another crazy idea, quite separate from the Bible. Can men fashion peace out of a wilderness of violence?

The current plan for peace in the Middle East, between

agitated Jews and angry Arabs, is a dream to many. The idea that ancient feuds can disappear is dismissed quickly by those weary of war and missed chances.

Few believe this literally means the end of all things, but the chances remain for a major regional conflict to escalate. In years past, Israel, long thought to possess nuclear capabilities, has officially declared that the state would simply "not be the first to use nuclear weapons," a veiled reference that, indeed, the Jewish state has developed a quite lethal arsenal.

In fact, perhaps the most worrisome scenario for international onlookers — particularly those in the West — is that if Israel finds its back to the wall, the "Samson Option" might be utilized. This apocalypse would be played out on a far wider scale than the biblical story of Samson, he of the superhuman strength who was finally taken prisoner by the Philistines. In the final act of his life, on display at a pagan festival, the Jewish hero toppled the pillars he was chained to, bringing the house down, as it were, on his tormenters. The idea that Israel might use its nuclear weaponry in such a modern-day scene is almost too frightening to contemplate.

In any event, even with the peace talks at a terrible impasse, peace itself doesn't have to be a dream. Those who have pursued peace know that a peace that works, such as the two-decade "cold peace" between Egypt and Israel, is a good thing.

It might be, though, that the formula mixed by the world community since the end of the Gulf War is fatally flawed. We shall see if the land-for-peace initiative is realistic or not.

For millenia, millions of Jews the world over have whispered to each other, "Next year in Jerusalem." The longing to return, en masse, from forced exile, has sustained this peculiar people. The story is told that former Soviet dissident Nathan Sharansky, when led away to prison, turned to his judges in the courtroom and said, "Next year in Jerusalem." This panting to return is difficult to understand, yet there it is.

Too, many Arabs have a connection to the land. These children of Ishmael have been here in some numbers much longer than the United States has been alive and thriving.

Today, a half-century after declaring statehood, the Jews of Israel find themselves in bitter negotiations with Palestinian Arabs seeking to establish their own state in that strip of land on the eastern Mediterranean.

The current attempts at bargaining are at once harrowing and tantalizing. The opportunities for peace are coldly clear to an entire planet thirsting for a respite from war.

As late as the week before Christmas 2000, with Bethlehem a virtual ghost town after months of clashes, the Palestinian National Authority's Minister of Jerusalem Affairs, Faisel Husseini, felt that a comprehensive peace agreement was near. The heightened bitter feelings between Jews and Arabs, brought on by daily skirmishes and terrorist acts, make this quest for a peace deal seem like a fairy tale.

Who are these two clans vying for supremacy in the Holy Land? This book aims to provide factual information for anyone confused by the issues between Israel and the Palestinian Arabs. We will deal with basic issues such as the identity of the Palestinian people, analyze Israel's neighbors and their history, review Jewish and Arab complaints of each other, peruse documents relevant to the peace process, and examine regional personalities.

It is a most fascinating story. The winds of history have never stopped blowing in this place, so far removed from the everyday experiences of Americans.

Let us hope, as one Israeli writer recently put it, that "the dogs of war" will go on sleeping. Peacefully.

ISRAEL'S "NEIGHBORHOOD"

ISRAEL

ISRAEL

CHAPTER ONE

THE
PLAYERS

Don't be embarrassed if you know little about the history of the conflict between Arabs and Jews; guilt over that is not useful to our discussion, so let's move on and start learning.

The modern nations in the Middle East are best understood initially by looking at a simple map (see preceding pages). Israel's size is much smaller than her neighbor's. All told, Israel's present landmass is approximately 10,000 square miles, compared to 5,414,000 square miles for the 22 Arab states.[1]

All the borders of these 23 nations were set within the last century. In antiquity, of course, the regional civilizations rose from the Babylonians, Assyrians, Greeks, and Romans. All of these powers were burdened by an ancient Jewish presence, which the biblical records tell us settled in the area in the second millenium B.C., forcing the Canaanites, for the most part, out of what is today the Mediterranean coastal regions, as well as mountainous areas of central Israel.

From that time to this, the land area between the Mediterranean Sea and the Jordan River has proven to be a popular travel and trade route between the Near East and the Far East. Countless armies have fought all through the

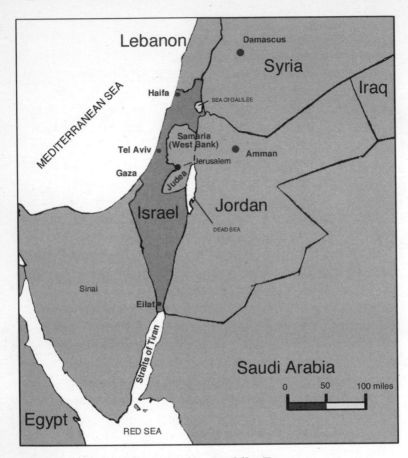

Present-day Middle East

region, from Egyptian pharoahs to the present-day participants of what is called the new *intifada* (Arabic for "liberation," or "shaking off").

Byzantine rule followed Rome, and then the burgeoning Islamic empire birthed by Mohammed in the early part of the sixth century fell on the region for several hundred years before being replaced by the Ottoman Turkish empire for four hundred years. In 1917, British field commander Lord Allenby took the storied city of Jerusalem from the Turks without firing a shot and the Holy Land, or Palestine, came under British rule.

After 30 years of attempting to mediate continuous fighting among Arabs and a growing Jewish population, the British effectively abandoned the area to the administration of the newly formed United Nations.

Much confusion exists regarding the name "Palestine." For Arabs, modern Israel is Palestine; for Israelis, the name is obsolete, except in a future peace treaty with the Palestinians as outlined in the Oslo accords.

The word "Palestine" derives from *Philistia*, the name given to the land of the Philistines. *Philistia* derives from the Hebrew term for the region.

For the Romans, who ruled the region for almost 400 years, the final Jewish rebellion under Roman occupation ended in A.D. 135. Henceforth, the emperor Hadrian renamed the country Palestina (in contrast to Judea), in order to wipe the last traces of Jewish influence from this hotly contested place.

From that date until 1948 the land was universally known as Palestine. On May 14, 1948, Jewish leader David Ben Gurion declared the establishment of the state of Israel.

A heavy influx of Jewish settlers into the area, beginning in the 19th century, began to have an effect on the local Arab population. Despite some pockets of cooperation and mutual goodwill (such as between Jewish and Arab leaders in 1919), outbreaks of violence began to occur. Finally, the 1948 declaration prompted an eruption when Israel's Arab neighbors publicly announced plans to invade the fledgling country.

The very next day, May 15, five Arab nations poured across the fresh borders. Heavy fighting all over the country gave way to a prolonged struggle, which eventually resulted in a cease-fire of sorts.

Flare-ups continued until the summer of 1967, when

Israel, confronted with heavy Syrian and Egyptian forces massed on the northern and southern borders, launched a preemptive strike. The lightning operation caught the Arab armies off guard; Israel's sweeping victory came to be known as the Six Day War. Suddenly, many biblical lands were back in Jewish hands, including the Golan Heights, Gaza Strip, Sinai Peninsula, and the West Bank (Judea/Samaria).

Interestingly, the term "West Bank" was coined by Jordan's King Hussein, in reference to a significant land area on the west side of the Jordan River. For more than 30 years, this has been disputed territory.

In 1973 the Syrians and Egyptians surprised the Israelis on the eve of the holiest day on the Jewish calendar — Yom Kippur, the Day of Atonement.

Only a tenacious effort by the Israelis and a daring tank maneuver in the Sinai saved Israel from being overrun. Since that time, no full-scale war efforts have been aimed at Israel, although the Persian Gulf War threatened to sweep over the entire Middle East.

Today, terrorist activities, and the consistent Israeli response, blanket the country on a daily basis.

WHOSE LAND?

Even those with only passing interest in the cauldron of Middle East politics know that in the last decade intensive efforts have been made to secure a lasting peace between Israel and the Arabs. This process of negotiations has come to be known as the Oslo accords, so named for the initially secret talks held in Norway between Israeli and Palestinian leaders.

For all its complexities, the Arab-Israeli conflict is most famous for the most basic of land disputes. Arabs claim that the Jewish state is illegitimate, built on Islamic land. Jews counter that the founding of the state was in accordance with U.N. approval.

A framework for peace, developed by American and

THE LAST WAR

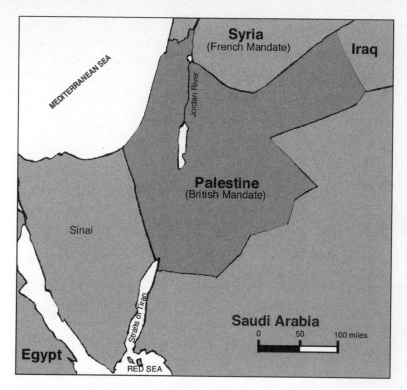

Palestine in 1920.

European diplomats, revolves around the idea of "land for peace." Israel is to have final, secure, recognized borders, while the Palestinian Arabs are to be given the opportunity to establish their own state, ostensibly on land in the West Bank and Gaza Strip, with connecting roads to be built.

It was at this point that negotiations broke down in July 2000 between Israel and the Palestinian National Authority and American mediators.

Israeli Prime Minister Ehud Barak, willing to go much further than previous heads-of-state in offering a comprehensive package to the Palestinians, was stunned when Palestinian National Authority (PNA) Chairman Yasser

Arafat rejected the proposal at a Camp David summit. Arafat had demanded that the Palestinians be given total sovereignty over Jerusalem's Old City, claimed since 1980 as Israel's capital.

Intensive talks consumed the last months of the Clinton administration, as a final peace accord was thought to be within grasp, bringing a historic peace.

Beyond this, many religious Jews claim an inheritance that dates from the time of the biblical patriarch Abraham. As the Genesis account goes, Abraham and his wife, Sara, were unable to have children of their own, so an Egyptian concubine, Hagar, produced Abraham's male heir, Ishmael.

In a twist that eclipses any Hollywood plot, Sara became pregnant and Isaac was born. The Bible indicates that the offspring of these two boys would be in perpetual disagreement, even violently so (Gen. 16:12).

Even many secular scholars trace the roots of this present-day conflict between Palestinians and Jews to this event. The sons of Ishmael — the Arabs — are at odds with the sons of Isaac — the Jews. The key to this is the reference to Isaac being the "child of the promise," that is, the land given to Abraham's seed by the Lord God would be a permanent gift to the Jewish people (Gen. 17:19). That the children of Ishmael were also given a rich inheritance (Gen. 17:20) is of little consolation to modern Arab nations.

Indeed, at the same time Jews lay eternal claims to the land, and in particular, the city of Jerusalem, the Palestinian Arabs make their own claims. A major effort is underway by Palestinian archaeologists to link this modern people with the Canaanites, Jebusites, and Philistines. Of course, this argument is based on a "we were here first" scenario.

A more modern dispute, however, has pushed the sacred story into an almost forgotten corner.

The question becomes this: was it just — even moral

— to establish a Jewish state in a sea of Arab countries?

Even before the Holocaust (Nazi Germany's plan to exterminate the Jews in Europe), numerous pogroms, or murderous vendettas, against Jewish populations in Russia and other places compelled key Jewish world figures to seek a safe haven for any Jew, anywhere in the world.

Theodore Herzl, a young Jewish journalist, covered the Dreyfus trial in Paris. The "Dreyfus Affair," as it came to be known, alarmed Herzl, who saw waves of anti-Semitism (hatred of Jews) wash over the trial and its aftermath. For the rest of his life, Herzl was a tireless champion of establishing a Jewish state, which would serve as a safe haven for Jews all over the world.

Thus was the movement known as Zionism born. Zionism, taking a cue from biblical references (Ezek. 37:25), is essentially the belief that the Holy Land is to be a Jewish possession forever.

Herzl was successful in obtaining some international support for his idea, although his premature death in 1904 prevented him from seeing the dream fulfilled.

As caretakers/occupiers after World War I, the British were at first sympathetic to the idea of a "Jewish national homeland." Leaders such as Lloyd George and Winston Churchill saw Palestine as the ideal place. Indeed, it is important to note that the Palestine of the early 20th century was a rather large landmass that eventually became the nations of Jordan and Israel (see map, page 23).

With the discovery and production of crude oil in largely Arab states, influential members of England's parliament and foreign service began to see the benefits of maintaining close contact with the Arabs. A shift in support from the Zionists to the Arab League was accomplished before the outbreak of World War II.

It is helpful, since this book aims to present basic facts, to identify just what Arabs and Jews are.

Although there have been attempts to link modern-day Palestinians with the Canaanites (and thus give the Palestinians the earliest title-deed, as it were), no compelling archaeological or cultural evidence exists to support the theory. What is known is that the **Arabs** as a distinct people began to emerge just after the time of Christ, the nomadic peoples following their herds of sheep across vast expanses of desert in the Middle East.

The Arabs came into real prominence with the introduction into history of Mohammed, who founded the religion of **Islam** in the seventh century, in the area of what is today Saudi Arabia.

Although the people of Iran, Lebanon, and Egypt are thought in the West to be Arabs, in fact, they are not. What unites these cultures is Islam.

Egypt, of course, is a very old civilization, one of the great centers of human activity in antiquity.

Iran itself was, until the last century, known as **Persia**. This equally impressive civilization rose from the fog of the distant past. In 1979 an Islamic revolution swept the country and the initial leader, Ayatollah Khomeini, declared himself to be an implacable enemy of Israel.

Right up to the present moment, Iran supplies radical Islamic terrorist organizations with money and other resources, and coordinates the activities of the Lebanon-based "Hizbollah" (the "party of God"). The Hizbollah is a terrorist group that has shelled communities in northern Israel for many years. In the summer of 2000, Israeli Prime Minister Ehud Barak made good on a campaign pledge to pull the Israel Defense Forces out of a "buffer zone" in southern Lebanon.

As for the **Jews** themselves, they are a distinct group also originating in the Middle East, with the Bible recording that God forged this nation from Abraham, sometime in the second millenium B.C.

After serving as slaves in Egypt for 400 years, the Bible says that the Israelites, under the direction of Moses and

THE LAST WAR

later his successor, Joshua, prepared to enter the land of Canaan.

Upon conquering large swatches of territory in what is today Israel and the West Bank, the Israelites continued a strong presence in the land, culminating in the reigns of David and his son, Solomon, with their capitals in Jerusalem.

This zenith of Jewish power began to wane two hundred years later as the powerful Assyrian empire (located in present-day Iraq) conquered the area. They were followed by Babylonian and Roman powers centuries later.

It is important to note that the Palestinians deny any Jewish presence in what some call the Holy Land, and archaeological excavations continue under the auspices of both peoples.

Perhaps the key "hot spot" in the entire region is the Temple Mount, so called by the Jews because two Jewish temples stood there, the last one having been destroyed by the Roman army in A.D. 70.

The Arabs know this hill in the heart of Jerusalem's Old City as Haram el al Sharif. Two Islamic shrines, the Al-Aqsa Mosque and the famous Dome of the Rock, occupy the site now.

Several key figures have entered and exited the stage of the Middle East in the past 50 years. Among the most important is Yasser Arafat, known to Arabs as Abu Ammar.

In 1968, four years after the founding of the Palestine Liberation Organization, Arafat became the leader of the PLO. Reviled internationally as a terrorist, Arafat maintained contacts throughout the Arab world, lived briefly in Jordan and Lebanon, then in exile in Tunisia, where he solidified his leadership of all the Palestinian people.

In the 1990s, Arafat suddenly found himself courted by diplomats and governments, as the United States and other Western countries rode the momentum of the Gulf War triumph to seek a comprehensive, lasting peace between Jews and Arabs in the Middle East.

By the time Israel officially recognized the PLO as the representative of Palestinian Arabs, Arafat had made the remarkable transformation into a statesman. Arafat's leap from leader of the Palestine Liberation Organization (founded in 1964) to chairman of the new, quasi-government known as the Palestinian National Authority was complete.

A succession of Israeli prime ministers — Yitzhak Rabin, Shimon Peres, and Benjamin Netanyahu — along with Barak, tried to finalize a permanent peace treaty with Arafat and his Palestinian National Authority.

All these leaders, and many others — on both sides of the dispute — have long believed that they would be the ones to lead the region down the path of peace. Sadly, each has found himself another stone in the pavement of a never-ending labyrinth of violence and social unrest.

Astonishingly, as Israel's early elections for prime minister loomed late in the year 2000, aging diplomatic veterans such as Peres and Ariel Sharon threw their hats into the campaign ring, underscoring the fluid state of Middle East politics.

Only months before, both Peres and Sharon, in their seventies, were thought to be too old to lead a changing nation into the future. Now they found themselves in viable positions.

Sharon, the military hero, and political pariah to some, visited the Temple Mount in Jerusalem on September 28, 2000, and media outlets the world over labeled the visit, following the lead of Arafat and the PNA, as a dangerous provocation.

Sharon, surrounded by a staggering number of Israeli security forces (1,000!) toured the site where two Jewish temples once stood. Now, two Islamic shrines, the Dome of the Rock and the Al-Aqsa Mosque, draw thousands of worshipers.

The cauldron of violence that had already spilled over erupted a day later as Palestinian militants exploited Sharon's hour-long visit. Into this bubbling stew the Israeli political scene cooked, while outgoing U.S. President Bill Clinton saw his chances for a historic peace agreement slip away.

As Texas governor George W. Bush made the transition to president, he named a foreign policy team (retired General Colin Powell, Stanford professor Condoleeza Rice, and others) that will no doubt keep many U.S. policies in place, as the superpower continues to try and find ways to mediate the dispute.

NOTES

1 Benyamin Netanyahu, *A Durable Peace: Israel and Its Place Among the Nations* (New York: Warner Books, 1999).

CHAPTER TWO

PALESTINE, OH PALESTINE

The romance of Palestine has been idealized in film and literature. Now it exists primarily in the realm of politics, and for many years there has been very little romance associated with this tiny patch of territory.

It is an astonishing fact of history that this land has found itself as the major prize in a colossal fight involving religious, political, and military factions.

Curiously, the Western mind wraps itself around the idea that Palestine existed once as a sovereign nation, teeming with, primarily, Arab intellectuals, businessmen, and desert nomads.

PALESTINE IN HISTORY

As has been mentioned, *Palestine* entered the language after A.D. 135. Those Jewish inhabitants not slaughtered by the Roman legions were expelled from the land, for the most part, although a Jewish population has remained in the land since Joshua's conquests in the second millenium B.C.

With the Moslem conquests beginning in the seventh century, various Arab groups have come and gone, as Palestine's rich countryside dried up.

Competing figures put the Jewish and Arab populations somewhere between unknowable and vague, but here are a few population statistics put forth from Jewish and Arab sources:

- The total population of Palestine a century ago was 500,000, of whom 47,000 were Jews who owned 0.5% of the land.[1]
- By the third quarter of the 19th century the total population of the entire country, Arabs and Jews, was still only 400,000.[2]

When one begins to dig into the history of the volatile modern state of Israel, one is struck by the contrasting versions of history from Jews and Arabs.

It is important to remember that as both groups make competing claims for the land, it is the Israelis who document history with places, dates, and names. The Arabs, on the other hand, those working overtime to establish a Palestinian right to the land, use prose and dreamy tales of ownership of the land.

The revising of history is a breathtaking thing to behold, especially on the grand scale we now see from the Palestinian leadership.

When direct military confrontation with Israel proved to be an unwise tactic, the Arab world — specifically Yasser Arafat's PLO — came up with an effective alternative to direct confrontation. A "right of return" concept had to be presented to the world.

Most people today assume that the "Palestinians" are an ancient nation, rooted out by the invading Zionist Jews shortly after World War II. Indeed, the plight of the fiercely proud Palestinians seeking a return to their homeland is constantly put before the public.

PLO spokeswoman Hanan Ashrawi, in her book *This Side of Peace*, constantly reiterates that her people are ris-

ing up against the brutal occupiers (the Jews) and demanding respect and a place at the international table:

> We had always lived with the conviction that
> the Palestinians were very important people be-
> cause of our human commitment and will, be-
> cause of our innate dignity as people of courage
> and destiny in harmony with our history and vi-
> sion.[3]

History?
The birth of the Palestinians as an Arab group displaced from their ancient homeland is a very recent inven-
tion.

Ashrawi also refers to heinous terrorist organizations
such as Hamas as "opposition groups," so one must question her objectivity on that basis alone. Hence, the need to
look into exactly what "Palestine" is.

Desiring to shake off any references to the trouble-
some Jews under its domain in the first century, Rome
changed the historic name of Judea (present-day Israel) to
"Palestina."

> While this Roman name disappeared in the
> land itself shortly after the conquest by the Mos-
> lems, Christian cartographers kept the name alive
> in their own lands and eventually bequeathed it
> to the Allied negotiators at Versailles and other
> inhabitants of the land, who adopted it only af-
> ter the British took control.[4]

Now an entire generation has slowly come to believe
that there has existed, at some point in the past, a nation
of "Palestinians," from Palestine. The West generally has
sympathy for oppressed groups (providing foreign aid,
church missions, humanitarian relief) and the Arab world

has cultivated such sympathy since Israel lost its underdog status in the miraculous Six Day War of 1967.

Since then, the false claim has been made over and over that Israel put a bayonet in the backs of helpless Palestinians, and drove them out of the country.

When Mark Twain (and others) recorded their visits to Palestine in the 1800s, they made it clear that the area was a gigantic boil on the globe. The land was unfit for habitation, much less being an object of national pride for "Palestinians."

In 1939, future U.S. President John F. Kennedy visited Palestine and recorded his thoughts of that event 20 years later in his book *The Strategy of Peace*. "In 1939 I first saw Palestine, then an unhappy land under alien rule, and to a large extent then a barren land." He marveled at the transformation a mere 12 years later, on his second visit:

> The transformation that had taken place was hard to believe. For in those 12 years, a nation had been born, a desert had been reclaimed, and the most tragic victims of World War II — the survivors of the concentration camps and ghettos — had found a home.[5]

And yet Yasser Arafat insists that the "Zionist invasion" rooted out his proud people, who were busy maintaining a thriving society.

In his 1993 book, *A Place Among the Nations*, Benjamin Netanyahu wrote:

> That Arafat is caught in another lie is by itself unimportant. What is important is that this lie, endlessly repeated, refined, and elaborated, has displaced what every civilized and educated person knew at the close of the nineteenth cen-

tury: that the land was indeed largely empty and could afford room to the millions of Jews who were living in intolerable and increasingly dangerous conditions in the ghettos of Europe who were yearning to return to the land and bring it back to life.[6]

Netanyahu went on to examine the evidence for this mysterious people, the Palestinians:

Who were the champions of the presumed Palestinian nation under the two centuries of Mamluk dominion or under the four centuries of Turkish rule? In what political organizations, social institutions, literature, art, religion, or private correspondence were expressed the ties of this phantom nation to that carved-up land? *None can be cited.* Throughout this long period the Arab inhabitants of Palestine never showed a hint of a desire for independent nationhood, or what is called today self-determination. There were Arabs who lived in Palestine, as elsewhere, but there was no such people as Palestinians, with a national consciousness, or a national identity, or a conception of national interests. Just as there was no Palestinian state, so too there was no Palestinian nation or culture.[7]

One can say that Netanyahu is lying, or just plain wrong about the history, but with a simple investment of time, *anyone can check it out.* In today's technologically advanced world, research resources are virtually limitless.

For example, when trying to get to the bottom of the Palestinian claim to the land, I browsed the worldwide web and stopped at the Palestinian National Authority (PNA) official website. You must understand that in order to bolster their claims to land in present-day Israel, the PNA must present cultural and historical evidence that "Palestinians" have inhabited the land for centuries, indeed, have "made it their own."

Scrolling through the list of options, I clicked on a site that displayed currency and coinage from Palestine. It is entitled, "Old Palestinian Currencies."

True enough, by clicking on any one of several examples, one can see currency from Palestine. But look closely and you'll see that the identification of the money is written in *Hebrew*, English, and Arabic. Just like street signs and so forth are listed today in Israel.

If anything, the currency shows that a Jewish presence has also existed in the territory once referred to as "Palestine."

The point is, Arafat and Company must *create* facts to bolster their claims to the land. They would like you to think that the Palestinian people had their own currency in 1927. If a 100-pound British note is the best they can do. . . .

As Netanyahu has said:

> Hence the principal effort of the ongoing Arab war against Israel since 1967 has been to defeat Israel on the battlefield of public opinion: in the media, in university lecture halls, and in the citadels of government.[8]

Perhaps the most important historical perceptions about the land are relatively recent, coalescing after the 1967 Six Day War. Until that time, the fledgling Jewish state was considered to be "David" to the Arab League's "Goliath." The characterization flipped after 1967, and a major effort was made to flesh-out the history of the Palestinian Arabs.

According to information found on the official internet website for the Palestinian National Authority, in

1967 "Israel launched a new war against the Arabs and seized the West Bank and Gaza Strip, the Syrian Golan Heights and the Egyptian Sinai Peninsula." Further, in the listing for 1973, "The October War between Israel and the Arab states broke out."[9]

These two entries are highly significant, for reasons we will explore.

Microfilm collections from these time periods are readily available to any researcher, along with the bottomless research well of the internet.

In 1967, Egypt's president, Gamal Abdel Nasser, making good on his numerous threats to "throw the Jews into the sea"[10] closed the Strait of Tiran and the Suez Canal to Israeli shipping, in defiance of international law. Finally, Nasser ordered U.N. peacekeeping forces out of the Sinai, setting the stage for some kind of confrontation with Israeli forces.

At the same time, Syrian troops began massing on Israel's northern border, aided heavily by control of the Golan Heights, a hilly region which enabled the Syrians to not only look directly on Israeli positions below, but to regularly shell civilian farmers and families.

In early June, Israeli intelligence detected massive troop movements on these southern and northern borders.

Israeli Prime Minister Levi Eshkol ordered the Israel Defense Forces to launch a preemptive strike at Arab military targets, beginning early on the morning of June 4.

Unprepared for this surprise maneuver, Arab forces scrambled to react. A stunning success rate all across the fronts enabled the Israelis to destroy the Syrian and Egyptian air forces, then rout the respective armies, in addition to engaging Jordanian forces in Jerusalem's Old City.

In less than a week, Israel had taken control of a staggering amount of territory — the Sinai, Gaza Strip, West Bank, and Golan Heights. Suddenly, tiny Israel now had defensible borders.

A little-discussed fact today reveals that Israel immediately offered to return the territory in exchange for formal peace treaties with the respective countries, but was rebuffed.

In retrospect, many in Israel today believe the swift victory instilled some sense of complacency in Israeli society. Thus, a mere six years later, the same major antagonists secretly prepared again to invade Israel.

On October 6, 1973, the eve of Yom Kippur, Syrian and Egyptian forces smashed into Israeli positions on the Golan and in the Sinai. Reeling, Israel desperately fought back.

The war stretched out for weeks, with Israel slowly repulsing all threats, and by the end of the month a U.S.-Soviet-brokered cease-fire took effect. Over time, the situation returned to what passes for normal in the Middle East, with a cessation of official hostilities, but with a return to continuous, low-grade terrorism.

For the purposes of our discussion, it is well worth noting the two PNA website references.

Consider that in the first reference Israel is named as

Ariel Sharon with Israeli troops during
the Yom Kippur War.

the aggressor, when in fact the Israelis did attack first, but to gain an advantage in a war aimed at Jewish annihilation. Secondly, when the Arabs attacked first, in 1973, the website references it benignly as "The October War between Israel and the Arab states broke out."

This fundamental rewording of historical reality has stained all subsequent attempts to hammer out peace agreements between Israel and the Palestinian Arabs, Syria, Iraq, and Lebanon. Thankfully, peace treaties with Egypt (1978) and Jordan (1994) have held.

After 1967, Arab intellectuals began circulating a history of Palestine that strangely appealed to Western diplomats and journalists, which at the same time flew in the face of simple facts. Into the world of investigative journalism swirled what some have called "Arabian Nights" stories.[11]

This battlefield has proven to be much more to the advantage of Arabs intent on creating a *judenrein* ("free of Jews") state.

Only Jews have spent thousands of years longing for *eretz* Israel — the "land of Israel." Only the Jews have ever made Jerusalem the capital of a nation.

It is puzzling to many why the Palestinian Arabs never made a move to establish an independent state in the years between 1948 and 1967 — the 19 years between the establishment of the state of Israel and the Six Day War. When east Jerusalem and the West Bank were controlled by Jordan, no Arab entity made a move to settle Palestinians there. Only since Israel has grown and prospered has the Arab world shouted about displaced Palestinians, Jerusalem as a capital, an independent state, etc. However, no media figure or world leader will ask questions like this of Arafat.

During the years between the world wars, international interest in establishing a homeland for the Jewish people intensified. In fact, Winston Churchill saw the heart of the matter in 1921:

It is manifestly right that the scattered Jews should have a national centre and a national home to be re-united, and where else but in Palestine, with which for three thousand years they have been intimately and profoundly associated? We think it will be good for the world, good for the Jews, good for the British Empire, but also good for the Arabs who dwell in Palestine . . . they shall share in the benefits and progress of Zionism.[12]

Zionism. That strange word is obscure to many Western minds, but in a nutshell it means the longing of Jews to return to the Holy Land and ancient Judea and Samaria.

Legendary Israeli general and current Prime Minister Ariel Sharon understands this connection to the land:

In my childhood fantasies I dreamed that even if the enemy came, the village would be invulnerable. Later, during the terrible first six months of the War of Independence [1948], I thought that even if the worst happened to the army, once the enemy arrived at the gates of the *moshav* they would not get through. Years afterward, when I was commanding a division in the 1967 war, I still had the same basic conviction. When the land belongs to you physically, when you know every hill and wadi and orchard, when your family is there, that is when you have power, not just physical power, but spiritual power. Like Antaceus, your strength comes from the land.[13]

Arafat has brainwashed millions of Arabs into believing the land belongs to the Palestinians. His lies are reinforced with subtle skill, as in his address on the Voice of Palestine radio, in Algiers, on December 31, 1993:

> Here is Palestine being reborn again as a national entity on its way to becoming an independent state.

Reborn again? And as a national entity? These are not mere fantasies, but a systematic crafting of public opinion away from historical facts.

Let's examine further the previously mentioned PNA website entry, "The October War between Israel and the Arab states broke out." Steering away from any verbosity here, the website merely records that a war did indeed break out between Israel and the Arabs. Never mind the fact that Egypt and Syria attacked Israel from the south and the north on the eve of Yom Kippur, the holiest day on the Jewish calendar.

The brief history for August 2, 1990, in which Iraq's Saddam Hussein swallowed Kuwait was tagged with this entry: "The Gulf Crisis erupted." It is the equivalent of the press in the former Soviet Union saying that during Stalin's exterminations of his own people "the Russian crisis erupted."

Certainly there were Arabs in the land when Israel declared independence in 1948. But this idea that Palestine belongs to the Palestinians and must be restored as a state is sheer fantasy. More than that, those in the PLO leadership know it is fantasy.

> It is only for tactical reasons that we carefully stress our Palestinian identity, for it is in the national interest of the Arabs to encourage a separate Palestinian identity to counter Zionism: The founding of a Palestinian state is a new tool in the ongoing battle against Israel.[14]

NOTES

1   Palestinian National Authority website.
2   Benyamin Netanyahu, *A Durable Peace: Israel and Its Place Among the Nations* (New York: Warner Books, 1999).
3   Hanan Ashrawi, *This Side of Peace: A Personal Account* (New York: Simon & Schuster, 1995), p. 286.
4   Netanyahu, *A Durable Peace*, p. 4 footnote.
5   John F. Kennedy, *The Strategy of Peace* (New York: Harper), p. 118.
6   Netanyahu, *A Durable Peace*, p. 40.
7   Ibid., p. 42.
8   Ibid., p. 81.
9   Palestinian National Authority official website, "A Brief History of Palestine."
10 Internet: ZDNetNews, "Talkback Central."
11 David Bar-Ilan, "Eye on the Media," *Jerusalem Post*, August 31, 1990.
12 Netanyahu, *A Durable Peace*, p. 48.
13 Ariel Sharon, *Warrior: The Autobiography of Ariel Sharon* (New York: Simon & Schuster, 1989), p. 25.
14 Zohair Mohsin, PLO Executive Council member, Trouw, Netherlands, March 31, 1977.

CHAPTER THREE

PEACE IN OUR TIME

Each year since the signing of the Oslo accords, the American Jewish Committee has conducted a survey of American Jewish opinion, as it applies to the peace process. An article in the *Middle East Quarterly* offered a chilling and insightful comment on the latest results of this poll:

> A careful examination of its results shows that American Jewry is increasingly wary of a negotiation process that it worries may be a trap for Israel.

In my 40 years of research into the Arab-Israeli conflict, I have never had more of a sense that Israel is in a dangerous place than I do today. The danger goes beyond the latest Palestinian uprising of 2000 2001.

Having never tasted defeat, Israeli generals might be confident of their chances in a regional war, but now Israel finds itself threatened not only militarily, but politically. This has shifted the balance of power away from Israeli superiority. It seems everyone feels that if Israel will make territorial compromises, her Arab neighbors will put away their weapons of war and their rhetoric, and settle down to life in a "new Middle East."

On August 20, 1998, U.S. President Bill Clinton faced a nationwide television audience to explain his decision to launch air attacks against Osama bin Laden's terrorist cells in Afghanistan and Sudan. This was in reaction to terrorist bombings of U.S. embassies in Africa one week before.

Reading from a prepared statement, the president said:

> I want you to understand, I want the world to understand, that our actions today were not aimed against Islam, the faith of hundreds of millions of good, peace-loving people all around the world, including the United States. *No religion condones the murder of innocent men, women and children.* But our actions were aimed at fanatics and killers who wrap murder in the cloak of righteousness; and in so doing, profane the great religion in whose name they claim to act (emphasis added).

The problem with this mindset is that the Koran, Islam's holy book, clearly and repeatedly states that followers of the religion — of Allah and his prophet Mohammed — are commanded to put to the sword anyone who resists conversion to Islam.

> Believers, take neither Jews nor Christians for your friends. They are friends with one another. Whosoever of you seeks their friendship shall become one of their number. God does not guide the wrongdoers (The Koran).[1]

Victor Mordecai, in his book *Is Fanatic Islam a Global Threat?* says that "Islam is a war religion."

When Yasser Arafat invokes the name of Allah in rallying Palestinian Arabs, he is binding himself in the confining robes of a religion that breathes the very definition of the word intolerance.

In writing about this threat, Mordecai says:

> According to Islam, there is an eternal war between the house of peace of Islam and the house of war of the infidel non-Moslem. Islam, in its early stages, adopted a strident ideology of war between "good and evil," i.e., Islam against the infidels. All who embrace Islam are of the House of Peace or, in Arabic, *Dar es el-Shalom*. All those who do not embrace Islam are of the House of War, or *Dar es el-Harb*. Muslims believe this war cannot end until the entire world is converted to Islam.[2]

The forces driving the Middle East peace process are not telling the truth to the world. A negotiated coexistence with Israel is not the goal. The goal is to use the peace process in bringing about a Middle East void of Jews.

If you find that hard to believe, brace yourself. The Herculean efforts by President Clinton, and many others like him, to find a formula for peace in the Middle East will fail miserably until we face the realities of those opposed to peace.

Europe in the 1930s was a simmering stew of nationalism, economic turmoil, and approaching war. Attempting to appease the expansionist German fuehrer Adolf Hitler was Neville Chamberlain, an earnest, dignified Englishman.

Chamberlain had been elbowed onto the international stage at a very dangerous time in history. Returning from a 1938 meeting with Hitler in Munich, the British prime minister waved to the crowd with a document he had signed with Hitler. Proclaiming that it represented "peace in our own time," Chamberlain felt he had satisfied the appetite of Nazi Germany by acquiescing to Hitler's demand for territory — namely the Sudetenland.

To make a long, bloody story short, Hitler's aims in his 1924 manifesto *Mein Kampf* came true as he brought war to Europe and the world at large. The appeasement-conscious Chamberlain died a broken man.

Another document with bloody goals surfaced in the 1960s. The Palestinian National Charter was drawn up and remains in effect to this day.

THE PALESTINIAN NATIONAL CHARTER

RESOLUTIONS OF THE PALESTINE NATIONAL COUNCIL, JULY 1–17, 1968

Article 1: Palestine is the homeland of the Arab Palestinian people; it is an indivisible part of the Arab homeland, and the Palestinian People are an integral part of the Arab nation.

Article 2: Palestine, with the borders it had during the British mandate is an indivisible territorial unit.

Article 3: The Palestinian Arab people possess the legal right to their homeland and have the right to determine their destiny after achieving the liberation of their country in accordance with their wishes and entirely of their own accord and will.

Article 4: The Palestinian identity is a genuine, essential, and inherent characteristic; it is transmitted from parents to children. The Zionist occupation and the dispersal of the Palestinian Arab people, through the disasters which befell them, do not make them lose their Palestinian identity and their membership in the Palestinian community, nor do they negate them.

Article 5: The Palestinians are those Arab nationals who, until 1947, normally resided in

Palestine regardless of whether they were evicted from it or have stayed there. Anyone born, after that date, of a Palestinian father — whether inside Palestine or outside of it — is also a Palestinian.

Article 6: The Jews who had normally resided in Palestine since the beginning of the Zionist invasion will be considered Palestinians.

Article 7: That there is a Palestinian community and that it has material, spiritual, and historical connection with Palestine are indisputable facts. It is a national duty to bring up individual Palestinians in an Arab revolutionary manner. All means of information and education must be adopted in order to acquaint the Palestinian with his country in the most profound manner, both spiritual and material, that is possible.

He must be prepared for armed struggle and ready to sacrifice his wealth and his life in order to win back his homeland and bring about its liberation.

Article 8: The phase in their history, through which the Palestinian people are now living, is that of national (watani) struggle for the liberation of Palestine. Thus the conflicts among the Palestinian national forces are secondary, and should be ended for the sake of the basic conflict that exists between the forces of Zionism and of imperialism on the one hand, and the Palestinian Arab people on the other. On this basis the Palestinian masses, regardless of whether they are residing in the national homeland or in diaspora (mahajir) constitute — both their organizations and the individuals — one national front working for the retrieval of Palestine and its liberation through armed struggle.

Article 9: Armed struggle is the only way to liberate Palestine. Thus it is the overall strategy, not merely a tactical phase. The Palestinian Arab people assert their absolute domination and firm resolution to continue their armed struggle and to work for an armed popular revolution for the liberation of their country and their return to it. They also assert their right to a normal life in Palestine and to exercise their right to self-determination and sovereignty over it.

Article 10: Commando action constitutes the nucleus of the Palestinian popular liberation war. This requires its escalation, and the mobilization of all the Palestinian popular and educational efforts and their organization and involvement in the armed Palestinian revolution. It also requires the achieving of unity for the national (watani) struggle among the different groupings of the Palestinian people, and between the Palestinian people and the Arab masses, so as to secure the continuation of the revolution, its escalation, and victory.

Article 11: The Palestinians will have three mottoes: national unity (wataniyya), national mobilization (qawmiyya), and liberation.

Article 12: The Palestinian people believe in Arab unity. In order to contribute their share toward attainment of that objective, however, they must, at the present stage of their struggle, safeguard their Palestinian identity and develop their consciousness of that identity, and oppose any plan that may dissolve or impair it.

Article 13: Arab unity and the liberation of Palestine are two complimentary objectives, the attainment of either of which facilitates the attainment of the other. Thus, Arab unity leads to the liberation of Palestine, the liberation of Palestine leads to Arab unity; and work toward the realization of one objective proceeds side by side with work towards the realization of the other.

Article 14: The destiny of the Arab nation, and indeed the Arab existence itself, depend upon the destiny of the Palestine cause. From this interdependence springs the Arab nation's pursuit of, and striving for, the liberation of Palestine. The people of Palestine play the role of the vanguard in the realization of this sacred (qawmi) goal.

Article 15: The liberation of Palestine, from an Arab viewpoint, is a national (watani) duty and it attempts to repel the Zionist and the imperialist aggressions against the Arab homeland, and aims at the elimination of Zionism in Palestine. Absolute responsibility for this falls upon the Arab nation — peoples and governments — with the Arab people of Palestine in the vanguard. Accordingly, the Arab nation must mobilize all its military, human, moral, and spiritual capabilities to participate actively with the Palestinian people in the liberation of Palestine. It must, particularly in the phase of the armed Palestinian revolution, offer and furnish the Palestinian people with all possible help, and material and human support, and make available to them the means and opportunities that will enable them to carry out their leading role in the armed revolution, until they liberate their homeland.

Article 16: The liberation of Palestine, from a spiritual point of view, will provide the Holy Land with an atmosphere of safety and tranquility, which in turn will safeguard the country's religious sanctuaries and guarantee freedom of worship to all, without discrimination of race, color, language, or religion. Accordingly, the people of Palestine look to all spiritual forces in the world for support.

Article 17: The liberation of Palestine, from a human point of view, will restore to the Palestinian individual his dignity, pride, and freedom. Accordingly, the Palestinian Arab people look forward to the support of all those who believe in the dignity of man and his freedom in the world.

Article 18: The liberation of Palestine, from an international point of view, is a defensive action necessitated by the demands of self-defense. Accordingly, the Palestinian people, desirous as they are of the friendship of all people, look to the freedom-loving, justice-loving, and peace-loving states for support in order to restore their legitimate rights in Palestine, to reestablish peace and security in the country, and to allow its people to exercise national sovereignty and freedom.

Article 19: The partition of Palestine in 1947 and the establishment of the state of Israel are entirely illegal, regardless of the passage of time, because they were contrary to the will of the Palestinian people and to their natural right in their homeland, and inconsistent with the principles embodied in the Charter of the United Nations, particularly the right to self-determination.

Article 20: The Balfour Declaration, the Mandate for Palestine, and everything that has been based on them are deemed null and void. Claims of historical or religious ties of the Jew with Palestine are incompatible with the facts of history and the true conception of what constitutes statehood. Judaism, being a religion, is not an independent nationality. Nor do Jews constitute a single nation with an identity of its own; they are citizens of the state to which they belong.

Article 21: The Arab Palestinian people, expressing themselves by the armed Palestinian revolution, reject all solutions which are substitutes for the total liberation of Palestine and reject all proposals aimed at the liquidation of the Palestinian problem, or its internationalization.

Article 22: Zionism is a political movement organically associated with international imperialism and antagonistic to all action for liberation and to progressive movements in the world. It is racist and fanatic in its nature, aggressive, expansionist, and colonial in its aims, and fascist in its methods. Israel is the instrument of the Zionist movement, and is the geographical base for world imperialism placed strategically in the midst of the Arab homeland to combat the hopes of the Arab nation for liberation, unity, and progress. Israel is a constant source of threat vis-a-vis peace in the Middle East and the whole world. Since the liberation of Palestine will destroy the Zionist and imperialist presence and will contribute to the establishment of peace in the Middle East, the Palestinian people look for the support of all the progressive and peaceful forces and urge them all, irrespective of their affiliations and beliefs, to offer the Palestinian people all aid and support in their just struggle for the liberation of their homeland.

Article 23: The demand of security and peace, as well as the demands of right and justice, require all states to consider Zionism an illegitimate movement, to outlaw its existence, and to ban its operations, in order that friendly relations among peoples may be preserved, and the loyalty of citizens to their respective homelands safeguarded.

Article 24: The Palestinian people believe in the principles of justice, freedom, sovereignty, self-determination, human dignity, and in the right of all peoples to exercise them.

Article 25: For the realization of the goals of this Charter and its principles, the Palestinian Liberation Organization will perform its role in the liberation of Palestine in accordance with the Constitution of this Organization.

Article 26: The Palestine Liberation Organization, representative of the Palestinian revolutionary forces, is responsible for the Palestinian Arab people's movement in its struggle — to retrieve its homeland, liberate and return to it and exercise the right to self-determination in it — in all military, political, and financial fields and also for whatever may be required by the Palestine case on inter-Arab and international levels.

Article 27: The Palestine Liberation Organization shall cooperate with all Arab states, each according to its potentialities; and will adopt a neutral policy among them in the light of the requirements of the war of liberation; and on this basis it shall not interfere in the internal affairs of any Arab state.

Article 28: The Palestinian Arab people assert the genuineness and independence of their national (wataniyya) revolution and reject all forms of intervention, trusteeship, and subordination.

Article 29: The Palestinian people possess

THE LAST WAR

the fundamental and genuine legal right to liberate and retrieve their homeland. The Palestinian people determine their attitude toward all states and forces on the basis of the stands they adopt vis-a-vis to the Palestinian revolution to fulfill the aims of the Palestinian people.

Article 30: Fighters and carriers of arms in the war of liberation are the nucleus of the popular army which will be the protective force for the gains of the Palestine Arab people.

Article 31: The Organization shall have a flag, an oath of allegiance, and an anthem. All this shall be decided upon in accordance with a special regulation.

Article 32: Regulations, which shall be known as the Constitution of the Palestinian Liberation Organization, shall be annexed to this Charter. It will lay down the manner in which the Organization, and its organs and institutions, shall be constituted; the respective competence of each; and the requirements of its obligation under the Charter.

Article 33: This Charter shall not be amended save by [vote of] a majority of two-thirds of the total membership of the National Congress of the Palestine Liberation Organization [taken] at a special session convened for that purpose.

In the charter's articles, multiple appeals are made to Arab unity in order to wipe Israel off the map. This outrageous document states clearly that a huge segment of the Arab world refuses to recognize Israel's very right to exist. Light mention is made of this in the press — usually implying that the Israeli government beats an irrelevant, outdated, dead horse by insisting on the Palestinian National Authority amending the charter.

At the conclusion of the October 1998 summit meeting in Wye, Maryland, Yasser Arafat promised (again) to strike from the PNA charter those offending sections calling for Israel's destruction. Congratulations and handshakes were offered all around by peace negotiators relieved that Arafat had compromised on the charter issue.

Although I will be accused of having a gloomy, misdirected outlook on this round of agreements, as a matter of conscience I must predict that not only will Arafat and the Palestinian National Authority (PNA) fail to keep various agreements, they will continue to directly threaten Israel with more acts of terrorism. If I stand alone in this conviction, so be it.

This and other instances of PNA non-compliance with the Oslo accords is met with yawns by media and heads-of-state representing their respective countries. This collective, Neville Chamberlain-like view of peace negotiations has brought the world to the brink of another tragic war.

To be sure, Israel has made mistakes since its inception. All nations do. But the systematic plotting of Israel's destruction by her enemies is one of the great stories of the age.

Unfortunately, the passage of time dulls anything we learn from history. Just as Neville Chamberlain felt he had crafted a lasting peace with a devilish despot, so, too, have we come to believe that Yasser Arafat intends to coexist peacefully with Israel, and nothing could be further from the truth.

The United States enjoys many advantages that are unique. Buttressed by the greatest natural defensive borders on earth, this superpower, still in its infancy, is unfamiliar with direct military threats.

Logically drawn to other experiments in freedom, the United States is friendly with many nations. One such kindred spirit is the state of Israel — a country constantly threatened with extermination.

This "national Jewish homeland" has been allied with

THE LAST WAR

the West since its birth in 1948, when the U.N. recognized Israel as a legitimate new neighbor in the community of nations.

And that's when the trouble really began.

Hated by her Arab neighbors, Israel found strong support from the United States, which both admired Jewish resiliency and kept an eye on self-interest, namely, oil. By helping maintain a balance of power in the Middle East, the United States could aid a friendly ally (Israel), while at the same time cultivate some type of "cold peace" with oil producers (various Arab states).

The modern history of the Middle East is a mixture of convoluted and painfully simple realities. On the one hand, the U.N. Partition Plan of 1947, in which "Palestine" would be divided between a Jewish state and an Arab state, was fairly straightforward in its goals. On the other hand, Arab nationalism, internal power struggles, and Israel's presence in the region have led to a Rubik's cube of military actions and political negotiation.

At the current heart of the problem, Israel is negotiating, with the United States as mediator, with an entity known as the Palestinian National Authority. The PNA is headed by Yasser Arafat, who until this decade was denounced worldwide as a terrorist. Today, he is received by heads-of-state everywhere, in large part because of peace negotiations initiated just after the Gulf War of 1991.

At the conclusion of that war, in which the United States and a coalition of several nations reversed the annexation of Kuwait by Iraq's Saddam Hussein, world leaders suddenly found themselves with a remarkable window of opportunity in the pursuit of peace in the Middle East.

U.S. Secretary of State James Baker brokered talks between Israel and her Arab neighbors. Secret negotiations had started earlier between members of Israel's Labor Party, and key Palestinian leadership. This series of talks, known as the "Oslo accords," took place in Norway.

Finally, in September 1993, Israeli Prime Minister Yitzhak Rabin shook hands with Arafat on the White House lawn and inked a deal to vigorously pursue peace. This Declaration of Principles outlined both Israeli and Palestinian obligations in the peace process, which centered on "land for peace." This agreement hinged on Israeli withdrawal from an unspecified percentage of territory obtained in a series of wars with Egypt, Syria, and Jordan.

In November 1995, a deranged Israeli, Yigal Amir, shot and killed Rabin immediately after a peace rally in Tel Aviv. As Shimon Peres succeeded Rabin, Arab terrorists sought to undermine the peace negotiations, setting off a devastating series of attacks on Israeli citizens.

The following May, Israelis elected Likud Party leader Benjamin Netanyahu as prime minister. The charismatic 47 year old ran a campaign based on his "peace with security" platform, and 60 percent of Jewish voters cast their ballots for Netanyahu.

Routinely introduced in the media as a "hardliner" and worse, Netanyahu constantly insisted that the Palestinians fulfill their responsibilities with regard to Oslo.

Daily in the press, Palestinians accuse Israelis of breaking agreed-upon pledges. Expectedly, Israelis accuse Palestinians of the same thing. Arafat publicly declares his desire for all of the West Bank (Judea and Samaria) and Gaza Strip (now under the control of the Palestinian National Authority). At the time of this writing, the "peace process" is considered comatose, even by its long-time supporters.

In the midst of all this, the superpower used to breathtaking natural borders is trying desperately to broker peace for an ally who has always known only narrow, dangerous borders.

By 1999, Netanyahu saw his hold on power slip away and former General Ehud Barak — Israel's most-decorated soldier — soundly defeated Netanyahu in summer elections.

The author with Prime Minister Benjamin Netanyahu
(1996-1999).

Underscoring the volatile nature of politics in the Middle East, Barak was himself unseated by challenger Ariel Sharon a mere 18 months later. One must wait to see what will develop from this latest event.

THE NEW MATH: 242 + 338 = 100%

In the new math of the Middle East peace process, numbers are manipulated to keep pace with Palestinian demands. Seeking a negotiated end to a pair of bloody, modern wars in Israel, the United Nations in 1967 and 1973 issued Security Council resolutions 242 and 338.

Israel — the victor in both wars with Arab neighbors — was required to give back "territories" taken in defensive actions. The Palestinians have convinced the world that the resolutions call for Israel to return *the* territories — all of them. And that is an issue of life and death. Just look at a map of Israel.

Following the Six Day War of 1967, in which Israel took control of the Old City of Jerusalem, the Golan Heights, the Gaza Strip, and the Sinai, the U.N. stepped in to formulate what was to become known as the blueprint for a negotiated settlement between the warring parties.

When that proved to be difficult at best, Resolution 242 simmered until Syria and Egypt attacked Israel in 1973. For weeks, Israel struggled to keep from being overrun, then managed to turn the tide. In fact, so miraculous was the victory, that Israel shattered the enemy armies. Again, the U.N. stepped in, with negotiations jointly conducted by the United States and the Soviet Union.

Today, Palestinians point to these two U.N. resolutions as being the centerpiece of an expected Israeli withdrawal to the pre-1967 borders.

Again, although the resolutions require that Israel withdraw from "territories," Arab radicals insist this means *all* territories claimed by Israel.

In the 1979 Camp David accords, agreed to by Egypt's Anwar Sadat, Israel's Menachem Begin, and the United States' Jimmy Carter, Israel relinquished control of the entire Sinai. Since that time, Israel has also withdrawn from Gaza, Jericho, Nablus, Bethlehem, Hebron, and other cities and towns.

Very few people in the West understand the territories being discussed. We hear words like "West Bank," "Gaza Strip," "Sinai," etc., and the understanding is not there. Hence, there is very little sympathy for Israel's plight, or outrage at the Arab's greed.

The withdrawals mentioned above add up to *93 percent* of the territories captured by Israel in 1967. Incredibly, the Palestinians demand all of it — 100 percent — to leave Israel with indefensible borders, borders that have been described as "Auschwitz lines."

They are so called because such borders would leave

the Jews with only one option: annihilation. Remember, even surrender and pacifism didn't satisfy the Nazis; extermination did.

It is almost impossible to describe Israel's precarious position to someone who hasn't been there. Let's try.

If you visit the country and land at Tel Aviv's Ben-Gurion Airport, the drive to Jerusalem takes all of 45 minutes. Just beyond Jerusalem is Jordan.

Should the Palestinians succeed in their plans to establish a state immediately east of the pre-1967 war borders, Israel will be ten miles wide at her narrowest point.

The West Bank, or Judea-Samaria to the Jews, consists of hilly terrain which has been used by invading Arab armies to fire on Israeli civilians and military personnel for decades.

This hilly country is literally a buffer against tank and infantry assaults, both of which Arab neighbors have demonstrated they are quite willing to use.

That is the point of this book: the Palestinian claims to hopes of coexistence with Israel are bogus. The goal is to secure land through political negotiations, then stage military operations designed to fulfill, say, the Palestinian National Charter. That's why the charter cannot be amended; it would discredit the very mindset of millions of Arabs.

To turn around an entire people from decades of murderous hatred would require more power than is currently available.

U.N. resolutions 242 and 338 were drawn up by people weary of unrest and war. But these flawed agreements are pointing a gun at Israel.

Yasser Arafat will be very happy to pull the trigger.

IS THIS ANY WAY TO TREAT TREATIES?

The difficult nature of seeking a resolution to the Israeli-Palestinian problem was underscored by the 1998 "Wye accords," which took place in Maryland.

Brokered by the United States, the event brought Benjamin Netanyahu and Yasser Arafat together for the first time in a long time. President Bill Clinton urged both sides to attend the Camp David-style summit, in order to hammer out some type of agreement.

Hosted at the Wye Plantation, the parties met for a grueling nine days, and despite the media hype, Israel and the Palestinians merely reaffirmed the salient points of previous agreements: further Israeli troop withdrawals from the West Bank, Palestinian crackdown on terrorism, etc. No new ground was really broken. However, the summit itself and the immediate aftermath reveal several gripping points:

- Arafat once again gave nothing but paper assurances.
- Israeli demands (again) for a revision of the Palestinian National Charter made only superficial headway.
- Israel continued to reiterate that no troop withdrawals would take place until the Palestinians gave concrete effort in fighting terrorism structures within areas they control.
- More terrorist attacks hit Israelis.

At Wye, Arafat pledged to basically welcome in a new era. Adding to the strangeness of his words in light of incitement to violence even after the summit, the media reported that the Palestinian leader rode a bicycle around the plantation grounds. He said that he hadn't been on a bicycle in many years.

The point of this little story is to show that Arafat was portrayed as a harried world leader who gratefully welcomes any opportunity to display some warm humanness, in contrast to the petulant, peace-bashing Benjamin Netanyahu.

The Israeli leader was reported to have threatened to

leave the summit and much was made of the Israeli team packing bags, which were then placed in a hallway. The Americans pursuaded Netanyahu to stay.

In other words, Arafat rides a bicycle, therefore, he's a peacenick; Netanyahu storms out amid a pile of suitcases when he doesn't get his way.

Look, any sane person desires peace and is hopeful any time adversaries meet in a civil atmosphere. We all fervently hoped Wye could be the basis of a lasting peace in the Middle East.

But it's a fantasy, a dreamland, when one side (Israel) is held to the fire, and the other side (the Palestinians) are not held accountable.

If you think the Wye summit held, or is holding the Palestinians accountable, consider these developments after the bike ride in the Maryland countryside:

Official Palestinian National Authority television aired the following on a religious program, November 3, 1998:

> There is no light nor teaching in their Torah [rabbinical commentary] today. Their Torah today is just a collection of writings in which those people wrote lies about God, His prophets and His teachings. The Jews are the seed of Satan and the devils. The Jews believe only in the first five books, which includes the Book of Genesis, all of which is lies about God and about the day of Creation. To their Prophets they attribute the greatest of crimes: murder, prostitution and drunkenness. The Jews do not believe in God, nor in the End of Days. They have distorted it [the Torah], lied about it and forged it. They invented it as a history book for the Jews, full of promises to Abraham, Isaac and Jacob that they would be given the land of Palestine. The entire Torah comes to demand ownership of the land

> for the Jews. Their history is full of rebellion and
> humiliation — God protect us from humiliation!
> They have distorted the faith and exchanged the
> gift of God for heresy, rebellion and prostitution,
> and distorted the Torah.[3]

Besides being painfully redundant, this broadcast is but one example of incitement against the Jews of Israel; there's more: During the first week of November 1998, Ahmed Tibi, an advisor to Arafat, announced on Israeli Television that the Palestinian National Council would not nullify the PLO charter.

Chief Palestinian negotiator Saeb Erekat said virtually the same thing a week before.

These are merely other examples of the Palestinians' contempt for summits, agreements, and implementations.

And still Israel is blamed.

Wye?

With little headway being made in peace talks in 1999, mostly due to Netanyahu's precarious position of power in Israel, the world waited for the match to light the Middle East powder keg. There seemed to be a sense of despair about the possibility that Oslo would bear any real fruit.

Barak's election victory compelled members of the various official peace camps to believe a comprehensive peace agreement between Israel and the Palestinians could be achieved in the near future, realistically speaking.

Indeed, Barak's far-reaching concessions (acknowledged by all sides) brought about a paradigm shift, however, in the hopes of Israeli citizens. Why?

All along, Arafat and his teams of negotiators told American mediators and the media that the Palestinians wanted, primarily, a state in the West Bank and Gaza Strip and a capital in east Jerusalem.

When U.S. President Bill Clinton immersed himself in the details of peace efforts, it became clear that the prin-

THE LAST WAR

ciples were headed for a summit of some kind. That finally happened in July 2000 when Clinton hosted Barak and Arafat at Camp David, the presidential retreat in the Maryland mountains.

Marathon discussions were held in which Barak astonished even liberal peace advocates in Israel and the United States by offering Arafat what seemed to all truly far-reaching concessions. These olive branches included what was once unthinkable: the Jews giving up control of the area surrounding its holiest shrines. No Israeli government had ever put the Temple Mount on the negotiating table, but Barak did.

As the world reeled with this news, Arafat's response to this unprecedented generosity on the part of the Israeli prime minister was even more shocking. Arafat said no!

Arafat refused any type of limited control of the shrines that occupy the same real estate in Jerusalem.

Although Barak offered the Palestinians 95 percent of the West Bank and Gaza Strip, recognition of such a state, and a foothold for a capital in Jerusalem, Arafat turned him down without so much as a counter-proposal. This angered the Americans and perplexed Israelis.

These events helped unravel Barak's fragile coalition, and by the time of Sharon's rise to the premiership several months later, even the most optimistic advocates of the peace process were in a funk. Suddenly the decade-long diplomatic dance seemed permanently frozen.

NOTES

1 Victor Mordecai, *Is Fanatic Islam a Global Threat?* (Taylors, SC: V. Mordecai, 1997).
2 Ibid.
3 Israel Government Press Office, Jerusalem, November 5, 1998.

CHAPTER FOUR

DREAMLAND'S NIGHTMARE

In his foreword to Samuel Katz' book *Battleground — Fact and Fantasy in Palestine,* Menachem Begin wrote:

> The [Arab] fabrication can probably most easily be seen in the simple circumstance that at the time the alleged cruel expulsion of Arabs by Zionists was in progress, it passed unnoticed. Foreign newspapermen who covered the war of 1948 on both sides did, indeed, write about the flight of the Arabs, but even those most hostile to the Jews saw nothing to suggest that it was voluntary. In the three months during which the major part of the flight took place — April, May, and June 1948 — the *London Times*, at that time [openly] hostile to Zionism, published eleven articles on the situation in Palestine in addition to extensive news reports and articles. In none was there even a hint of the charge that the Zionists were driving the Arabs from their homes. . . .
>
> Our struggle for peace and for the security of our people seems to be still far from ended. In a world in which pragmatic interests — such as

the thirst for oil or for petrodollars — seem to play an overriding role it may be thought by some that mere facts, mere truth, are pale competitors. Yet for our people whose God's name is Truth — "for He is truth and His name is truth" — we shall continue to use truth as a main weapon.[1]

While gathering material for this book, I shared a delightful evening meal with my friend, Ya'akov Kirschen, the Israeli cartoonist of *Dry Bones* fame. As the sounds of nighttime Tel Aviv melded into our conversation, he hit on the crux of the problem:

> If you can say to people, "Where are the problems in the world?" People would say, "Well, there are problems in Chechnya. There are problems in Serbia, Croatia, Bosnia. There's fighting going on in India. There are problems in the Philippines. There are problems in Sudan. There are problems in the Middle East." What's interesting is that each of those isolated problems is a battle between Islamic and non-Islamic people. Chechnya is a war between Moslems and Christians. In the Middle East it's a war between Moslems and Jews. In India it's a war between Moslems and Hindus. In the Philippines it's a war between Moslems and Christians. That's the same as if the media was looking at World War II and saying, "Oh, there's a battle going on with Russia, there's a battle going on with France, there's a battle going on with England, there's a battle going on with Japan." And then you say, "Well, you dummy, it's World War II, of course." Each of those things is simply an area of battlefield, but it is not the *whole* story. It's only a little piece of the story. The story is, it's World War II. And

as we are looking at our situation today it seems
to me the story is the great jihad [holy war]. The
story is that the forces of Allah are moving to
extinguish the Jews and the Christians. The media which is largely Christian and Jewish simply
refuses to recognize it.

Now that really is a big problem.

To be sure, there are peace-loving people in the Moslem world. This book is not a polemic against those who
genuinely want peace. I have had the privilege of having
peaceful dialogue with people on both sides of the conflict.

The problem — the threat to us all — comes from radical elements who have gone down the road of hate.

So Kirschen's words must be heard. The issue must
be addressed. His comment is not one of bias; it is historical fact — history that we are living right this moment.

The late Syrian leader Hafez Al Assad, as a murderer,
was cut from the same cloth as Hitler and Stalin. That he
has not murdered on the scale of those two is simply due to
geography and placement in history. Dictators always lay
waste to territory under their control, and Assad was no different. You will rarely, however, hear any media figure con-
demn Assad. Consider this quote from Thomas Friedman:

> It is not only in internal affairs that the Syr-
> ian government has elevated extremist violence
> to an instrument of state. During 1980 and 1981,
> Syrian agents went on the offensive in Beirut,
> shooting and killing several Lebanese and West-
> ern journalists in order to discourage reporters
> from writing negatively about Syria. As a mem-
> ber of the press corps at the time, I can testify
> that the campaign had its intended effect. Al-
> though unflattering stories about Syria still go
> out, there wasn't a journalist in Beirut who didn't

think twice, or even three times, about writing ill of the Syrian regime.[2]

Syria has been linked to countless acts of terrorism around the world, including the 1983 bombing of the U.S. Marine barracks in Beirut, yet today this dictatorship is warmly embraced as a peace partner. It is worth noting that Assad never gave an indication that he sought genuine peace.

The West's short attention span pushes heinous acts of terrorism into such dark, hidden corners that they are forgotten except for the families of the victims.

In the 1973 Yom Kippur War, Syrian forces captured 28 Israeli soldiers. What was the fate of these POWs? The Syrian *Official Gazette* of July 11, 1974, has the account of these 28 Israel Defense Forces soldiers.

> There is the outstanding case of a recruit from Aleppo who killed 28 Jewish soldiers by himself, slaughtering them like sheep. All of his comrades-in-arms witnessed this. He butchered three of them with an axe and decapitated them. In other words, instead of using a gun to kill them, he took a hatchet to chop their heads off. He struggled face to face with one of them and throwing down his axe managed to break his neck and devour his flesh in front of his comrades. This is a special case. Need I single it out to award him the Medal of the Republic? I will grant this medal to any soldier who succeeds in killing 28 Jews, and I will cover him with appreciation and honor for his bravery.
>
> General Mustafa Tlas, Minister of Defense
> 12th Session of Parliament
> December 1, 1973.[3]

Where is Mustafa today? He is still head of defense for Syria.

Sadly, when Assad died suddenly in 2000, his hand-picked successor, his son, Bashar, seemed intent on not only continuing the policies of his father, but the younger Assad even opened channels of communication with Iraq's Saddam Hussein!

The point of all this is, a terrorist like bin Laden is partnered with the Assads and Arafats of the world, dedicated to killing as many Westerners as possible.

When you read the newspapers and watch television news, don't forget that the goals of radical Arab states regarding Israel and the United States are the same.

Few remember the 1973 murder of U.S. Ambassador to Sudan, Cleo Noel. His death came at the hands of Black September, a terrorist group headed by Yasser Arafat.

Obviously, Arafat not only escaped punishment, but he is kissed and hugged by world leaders today. How sad that the passage of time further cheapens the lives of people like Cleo Noel.

Terrorist organizations constantly vie for supremacy, and there is serious infighting among them. For example, George Habash's Popular Front for the Liberation of Palestine is at odds with Arafat and his PLO factions. Syria's Assad had a long history of ordering the assassinations of those within the Arab world that he considered threats.

However, the basic goals remain the same: eliminate Israel, *the little Satan* and eliminate the United States, *the great Satan.*

It is astonishing to watch the worldwide apathy today to such realities.

Thank God for a man like Joseph Farah, who is a Christian-Arab journalist whose pro-Zionist viewpoint is like a breath of fresh air in this world of stale ideas such as embraced by the majority of the Western media. He wrote the following letter:

An Open Letter to Arafat

Dear Mr. Arafat:

I couldn't help but notice that your recent rhetoric, as in your speech to the Arab Summit last week, suggests you are now not only a self-proclaimed spokesman for the "Palestinian people," but for Christian interests in the Middle East as well.

Here are some of the recent references [Arafat's] that piqued my curiosity:

• "The blood that was shed in Al-Aqsa definitely unleashed the wrath in the hearts of our Palestinian masses everywhere in the homeland. The unarmed citizens rose to express their feelings in a legitimate spontaneous intifada to uphold Arab, Islamic, and Christian values in accordance with the Umarite Covenant. The Israelis canceled this covenant, by claiming sovereignty over Al-Haram El sharif and forging its history and reality and saying it is the place where the Temple was built, by licentiously attacking the worshipers in its mosques and those defending its honor and sanctity, or by attempting to Judaize holy Jerusalem and its Christian and Islamic holy places and imposing a siege on Bethlehem."

• "Our people of revolutionary struggle, the people of the glorious intifada, whose waves will only stop with victory, pledge to every Arab, Muslim, Christian, and friend to continue their struggle using all legitimate means to reach victory."

• "Let me tell you something. The issue of Jerusalem is not just a Palestinian issue. It is a Palestinian, Arab, Islamic, and Christian issue."

• "Let us begin from the holy Buraq wall. It

is called the holy Buraq wall, not the Wailing Wall. We do not say this. After the holy Buraq revolution in 1929 . . . the Shaw International Committee said this is a holy wall for Muslims. This wall ends at the Via Dolorosa. These are our Christian and Muslim holy places."

I recently spoke out as an Arab-American in opposition to your tactics and goals, Mr. Arafat. Today, I speak out against them as a Christian.

Let me be blunt: Despite extensive travels throughout the Middle East, I have not met a single Christian Arab who did not have misgivings about you. I certainly have never met one who considered you a representative of his interests in the Holy Land. In the United States I have never met a Christian who thought you were anything but an anti-Jewish terrorist. That's the way I think of you.

You may indeed actually represent many of those rioting in the streets of Ramallah and Gaza and Jerusalem, but you will never speak for Christians anywhere — not real Christians, not followers of the Lord Jesus Christ, who was, you might recall, a Jewish rabbi.

By definition, Christians must reject your agenda of hate and genocide.

In addition, Christians old enough to remember what access to the holy sites was like under Islamic rule are hardly eager to support your cause in Jerusalem. We know where that leads. Jews may be your number one enemy today. We know Christians will be next.

Mr. Arafat, you may have fooled enough people in elite circles to have won yourself millions in U.S. taxpayer aid and even a Nobel Peace

Prize. But all you have really managed to do with those victories is to diminish and corrupt the meaning of those awards.

Sincerely,
Joseph Farah
A Christian Arab-American who supports
the Jewish state[4]

Perhaps a more terrifying threat than murder would get the attention of U.S. citizens. Anyone old enough to remember the oil embargo of 1973, in which Arab countries punished the United States for its support of Israel during the Yom Kippur War, dreads the thought of more gas lines, shortages, and giving up luxury cars.

NOTES

1   Samuel Katz, *BattleGround: Fact and Fantasy in Palestine* (New York: Steimatzky/Shapolsky, 1985), p. x–xii.
2   *New York Times* magazine, October 7, 1984.
3   Yitschak Ben Gad, *Politics, Lies and Videotape* (New York: Shapolsky Publishers, 1991), p. 366–367.
4   Joseph Farah, "An Open Letter to Arafat," October 24, 2000, <http://www.worldnetdaily.com/bluesky_btl/20001024_xcbtl_an_open_le.shtml>.

IS THE MEDIA
BIASED?

Ancient Israel attracted many enemies in a quest for a homeland. Among the most savage foes the Israelites engaged were the Midianites, an implacable enemy from the east.

Wherever they have wandered through the passing centuries, the Jews have encountered furious opposition. That proclivity unfortunately has passed to generations of sons and daughters.

Today, the enemy's spears, arrows, and shields have morphed into pens, computers, and the first amendment. And make no mistake: today's "media-ites" stand a much better chance of wiping Jews off the map than the ancient Midianites.

The modern-day enemies of Israel employ a variety of weapons in this endeavor, and when the media wants to do a hatchet job it is usually able. Perhaps the chief weapon is one that leaves no traces. It is the Phantom Story.

In November 1997 a syndicated American columnist wrote a piece implying that Israeli Prime Minister Benjamin Netanyahu had put his foot down on the tail of that eager, endangered animal, "the peace process."

Taking Netanyahu to task for single-handedly block-ing the road to peace in the Middle East, the writer built up a thick, if factually lean, litany of abuses by Netanyahu.

But then a monkey-wrench was thrown into the whole tirade. Drawing parallels between Bill Clinton and Netanyahu, the writer mused:

> In neither does one find tactical or strategic coherence or military experience (neither, for instance, served in their respective armies); in both of them, shallowness has reached new depths.

This is shocking to those who thought they served with Netanyahu for five years in an elite Israeli commando unit. It is shocking to those who trained him, shocking to his family, and most shocking to the terrorists he helped capture.

Before this brazen announcement of Netanyahu's blank military career, it was widely known that he had served with distinction. In point of fact, all able-bodied Israelis serve a stint in the military, and have since the creation of the state in 1948.

The perception of Netanyahu as a military hawk, without his own military experience, is damaging, since readers shape their opinions based on the media. The column implied that Netanyahu's negotiating strategies were illegitimate, given his "lightweight career."

Barak himself was considered the darling of the left when he ascended to power in 1999, but soon found that he couldn't please anyone. No doubt, such a target as Sharon will invite withering criticism, no matter his course of action.

Back to the Netanyahu savaging.

Besides seeing action himself, Netanyahu lost his brother, Jonathan, during the raid on the Entebbe airport in Africa in 1976, after PLO terrorists had hijacked a planeload of Israelis. In fact, the Netanyahu family set up the Jonathan Institute, a think-tank for studies in terror-

ism prevention, in memory of their fallen son.

Since the Six Day War of 1967, Israel has seen itself transformed in the world media from a 98-pound weakling into a regional bully, herding hapless Palestinians into refugee camps and "occupying" Arab lands.

David Bar-Illan, director of policy planning and communications for Israeli Prime Minister Benjamin Netanyahu, has long tracked media bias against Israel. His 1993 book *Eye on the Media* is a compilation of some of his columns during his stint as editor of the *Jerusalem Post*.

In an October 1990 column, Bar-Illan noted two examples of biased reporting against Israel:

> The London newspaper, *The Independent*, headlined its page one report on the Abul Abbas raid on the Tel Aviv beaches with "Israelis kill four Palestinians on beach." This is in reference to a boat assault by terrorists, aimed at Israeli civilians, in which the Israeli Defense Forces intervened.

Bar-Illan also took a look at American television anchors:

> ABC's glamorous anchorman Peter Jennings, a pioneer in the slanted news business, is much more subtle. He once introduced a report about an Arab terrorist stabbing two elderly Jews to death with "An Arab was almost lynched by a Jewish mob in Jerusalem today."

Such is the experience of the Israelis, who struggle to see objective reporting of their country. As Bar-Illan has said, "Give me a news story about Indonesia, and I'll believe every word. Give me one about my neighborhood, and I'll have trouble finding a single accurate detail."

When a deranged Jordanian soldier shot and killed seven Israeli schoolgirls on an island in the Jordan River in 1997, the *New York Times'* Anthony Lewis wrote an astonishingly vitriolic op-ed piece.

Admitting in the column's opening paragraph that, indeed, a Jordanian was actually responsible for the shootings, Lewis then spent 13 paragraphs lambasting Benjamin Netanyahu for holding up the peace process and "shattering" the hopes of Palestinians for their own homeland. None of this had anything to do with seven Jewish girls being brutally murdered on a school outing.

Why shift the focus of a heinous murder to criticism of Israel? Because the goal of influential members of the media is to build support for a state of Palestine. But as an editorialist for the *Detroit News* has noted, "Considering the large Arab population in Detroit, one must admire the *Detroit News'* editorials in particular. Following is an excerpt: 'If Secretary Baker is looking for a quick solution, there is one available. A Palestinian state already exists in the Middle East: Jordan. Rather than beating on Israel to render itself militarily indefensible, why not put the heat on King Hussein of Jordan who backed Saddam in the Gulf War, to deliver on a homeland?' "[1]

The cover story of *Time* magazine for June 10, 1996, focused on Netanyahu's election victory over Shimon Peres. Inside the magazine, former U.S. Secretary of State James Baker was quoted as saying the election results were "a major setback for the peace process." This leaves the reader with the impression that Netanyahu collapsed the peace process, but the discerning reader will note that what the multitude of quotes like Baker's really mean is: Netanyahu collapsed the peace process before he took office. Of course, that is clearly impossible, because it would be quite difficult for a candidate to set policy.

The reality is that in March 1996, six months after Yitzhak Rabin's assassination and Peres' ascent to power,

Arab terrorists killed 56 Israelis in a span of nine days, in hopes of derailing the peace process.

So, the question must be asked: Which is more dangerous to the pursuit of peace, a democratic national election, or bloodthirsty terrorists?

The incessant media drumbeat that Netanyahu, Sharon, and even Barak (and other Israelis concerned about the land-for-peace initiative) are so intransigent that the peace process is held hostage by them and them alone, continues unabated. This is logically preposterous, but what is more preposterous is the fact that so many readily accept this media distortion.

And it works. Now that Prime Minister Ehud Barak's left-wing government had its crack at leading Israel, it is even more evident that these tactics do work. Mr. Barak bent over backwards to try to please Arafat and the Palestinian National Authority. His failed policy of giving more and more "land for peace" had many Israelis alarmed. They feared abandonment of the Zionist dream. They were afraid that Barak and company were ready to "give away the farm." For sure, if the Palestinians have their way, Israelis will give away all of the land retaining only a small plot measuring 3' x 6' x 6' per person.

According to the Committee for Accuracy in Middle East Reporting in America (CAMERA), the *Washington Post* published an insightful op-ed article by Charles Krauthammer (1987 Pulitzer Prize winner, columnist for the *Washington Post*).

CAMERA commented, "While the *Washington Post* has done very little news reporting about the ubiquitous anti-Israel, anti-Jewish emissions from Israel's peace partners, we were very pleased to note that the *Post* published an informative column (see below) on this topic from Charles Krauthammer entitled, "The Peace of the Anti-Semites." This article appeared in the *Washington Post* on Friday, January 7, 2000, on page A23:

On Jan. 4, Israel signed an agreement giving up yet another block of West Bank territory to the Palestinian National Authority. A week earlier, the official Palestinian National Authority newspaper, *Al Hayat Al-Jadida*, ran a cartoon. . . . The old man is labeled "the 20th century," the young man "the 21st century." The dwarf standing between them and wearing a Jewish skullcap and a Star of David is labeled "the disease of the century."

Blessed are the peacemakers.

On the other "peace" front, Israeli Prime Minister Ehud Barak meets with the Syrian foreign minister in Shepherdstown, W.Va., to negotiate Israel's giving up the Golan Heights, which protect Israel's northern frontier from Syrian tanks. Just a few weeks earlier, in the Damascus weekly of the Syria Arab writers' association (*Al-'Usbu' Al-Adabi*), the following appeared:

> The Talmud's instructions, soaked in hatred and hostility towards humanity, are [stamped] in the Jewish soul. Throughout history, the world has known more than one Shylock . . . more than one Toma as a victim of these Talmudic instructions and this hatred.

Peace be with you.

Toma is the Capuchin missionary, Father Thomas, who was murdered in Damascus in 1840. The Jews of Damascus were accused of having killed him to use his blood in Passover matzohs.

This blood libel is one of the oldest and most insane medieval fantasies about Jews. Centuries ago it was believed enough that many Jews were murdered on its account. In our era, those who continue to purvey it are either lunatics or Syrians. It is not just their writers. In 1984, a book called *The Matzoh of Zion* was published in Damascus — with a preface defending the 1840 blood libel as truth, written by Mustafa Tlas, Syria's minister of defense! In 1991 the Syrian delegate to the U.N. Commission on Human Rights urged the commission to read the book in order to learn the "historical reality of Zionist racism."

When in the United States, Syrian spokesmen don't bring up blood libels. (It was the Middle East Media and Research Institute that discovered the revival of the Father Thomas incident.) They speak soothingly instead of their deep desire for "the peace of the brave." Looking at what their leaders tell their own people about Jews, however, one gets the distinct impression that their ultimate goal is the peace of the grave.

These campaigns of anti-Semitism — not anti-Zionism, as some pretend, but raw, brute anti-Jewish calumnies — are commonplace in the Arab world, particularly in the state-controlled Palestinian, Syrian, and Egyptian press. Americans got an accidental glimpse of the virulence of this hatred during Hillary Clinton's visit to Israel last November [1999] when Suha Arafat accused Israel of causing cancer in Palestinian women and children by means of poison gas.

Media attention focused on Clinton's lack of response. The real story, however, was this glimpse at the savagery of the Arab elite's commonplace discourse regarding Jews and Israelis.

This, after all, was not some ignorant functionary speaking, but the first lady of Palestine.

And it raises a very acute question: What type of peace do such people — who call Jews the disease of the 20th century, who claim that Judaism commands the slaughter of Gentiles for the ritual purpose of eating of their blood — really have in mind?

The optimists, or call them fantasists, led by the Clinton administration simply ignore these manifestations of pathological bigotry. They insist that the peace that Arafat and Assad want to make with the perfidious Jews would be a permanent one.

Ehud Barak, no fantasist, is quite familiar with the press of his neighbors and what it preaches about Jews. Which is why he is trying to obtain a peace, both with Syria and the Palestinians, that will leave Israel with enough territory, enough strategic depth, enough defensible positions to be able to withstand a renewed war in case the Arabs find their hatred for Jews not quite fully assuaged by paper agreements.

Bill Clinton is another matter, however. He is in desperate search of a legacy. And that for him means an agreement — any agreement — that he can trumpet on the White House lawn. He doesn't really care about its shape and content. He wants the ceremony.

But there is another legacy at stake in these negotiations. And that is the legacy of the 5 million Jews who live in Israel. Who in turn carry the legacy of the 6 million who died in the Holocaust, and of the countless others martyred over the millennia.

Their legacy is to bequeath to future gen-

erations a reborn Jewish state that can defend itself. When push comes to shove in the negotiations, their desire for a secure future will come into conflict with Clinton's desire for an ostentatious diplomatic success. The question for Clinton is whether he will have the statesmanship to subordinate his personal political needs to the more enduring needs of an enduring peace.

(Copyright 2000, *The Washington Post Company*)

Middle East analyst and commentator Emanuel A. Winston contends that misinformation about the Arab-Israeli conflict is a harsh reality. He wrote in July 1998:

> The objective of this continuing campaign is to fire up the media, and through them, the American people, with the idea that, through a carefully constructed revision of history, Jerusalem does not belong to the Jews but rather to Arafat's Palestinians.[2]

Sure enough, an August 5, 1998, Associated Press article announced the discovery of an ancient city identified as Canaanite, by Palestinian archeologists working near the present-day city of Nablus, in the West Bank.

Since there is universal agreement that Canaanites predated Jews in that area of the world, Arafat desperately needs to link himself and his people with Canaan.

There are two problems with the archeologists' contentions, as outlined in the AP article:

> One, there is no way at all to confer descendence from Cannanites on today's Palestinians; the former's disappearance into history is as murky as the rise of the new Palestinians.

Secondly, the city of Nablus carries an Arabic name that came into being in this decade. Before that, the site was named Shechem, a decidedly Hebrew name.

In December 1999 the Israelis permitted the Palestinians to begin constructing a new entrance into a Moslem prayer room under the Temple Mount. One result of this decision was the removal of tons of dirt containing remnants of the two Jewish temples. The dirt was dumped in a nearby valley, which technically precludes any artifacts found as belonging to the Jewish holy sites. This allows Arafat's state-controlled media to declare that the Jews have no basis for their claims to the Temple Mount.

The lastest Palestinian uprising, which began in September 2000, is given favorable coverage by most media outlets. While the Arabs certainly have historical and religious claims to their own shrines, it is disturbing in the extreme that Jewish longing for freedom of access to these sites is seriously undermined.

This is but one aspect of the whole convoluted affair; a chief reason why a permanent peace agreement between the two sides — as it stands now — might be impossible.

NOTES

1 David Bar-Illan, *Eye on the Media* (Jerusalem: Jerusalem Post, 1993), p. 154.
2 Gamla website, July 1998.

CHAPTER SIX

WHO IS YASSER ARAFAT?

A new villain in news stories about terrorists is Osama bin Laden, the Saudi Arabian millionaire living in, well, various parts of the world. On a PBS broadcast, Osama bin Laden spoke very frankly about the goals of Islam:

> I am one of the servants of Allah. We do our duty of fighting for the sake of the religion of Allah. It is also our duty to send a call to all the people of the world to enjoy this great light and to embrace Islam and experience the happiness in Islam. Our primary mission is nothing but the furthering of this religion. . . . Let not the West be taken in by those who say that Muslims choose nothing but slaughtering. Their brothers in East Europe, in Turkey and in Albania have been guided by Allah to submit to Islam and to experience the bliss of Islam. Unlike those, the European and the American people and some of the Arabs are under the influence of Jewish media.[1]

We are to understand by his statement that bin Laden is not interested in slaughtering those who bow to Allah and become good Muslims. Only those who refuse his overture to join the ranks of the followers of Mohammed are to be murdered in a religious frenzy that can countenance no difference of opinion.

How often do you hear Osama bin Laden linked to Yasser Arafat or Saddam Hussein? Although they have the same goals, strategies, and ideologies, bin Laden is, deservedly, a pariah among the world's civilized peoples. Look at what this rich veteran of the Afghanistan War does with his time:

- funds terrorist activities around the world
- unleashes hate-filled diatribes against the West
- incites his followers to violence

Now, if you care to spend a little bit of time investigating these other two men — Yasser Arafat and Saddam Hussein — what would you find?

- they fund terrorist activities around the world
- they unleash hate-filled diatribes against the West
- they incite their followers to violence

So why is bin Laden public enemy number one, while Arafat is a statesman, and the late Hafez al Assad, as described in a *Time* article, "a hard-eyed sphinx? [read: worthy of grudging respect, if not admiration]"

Despite varied efforts to portray Islam as a benign religion that is unfortunately sullied by the loose-cannon reputations of a few stray thugs, it is a religion based on conquering by violence and force. Read the Koran. Read the history of Mohammed, the founder of Islam. Whether Islam is used as a religious war club, or incorporated into the political strategies of rogue leaders is really beside the point.

When bin Laden vows to destroy Jews and Americans, and Arafat vows to do the same thing, they are speaking the same language. They are brothers in the war against the great Satan, America, and the little Satan, Israel.

Because Saudi Arabia allows U.S. troops on its soil, we think of them as allies. The Saudis, however, feel little love for Americans. Even if the ruling party there wanted to accommodate American military intervention in the region, such as during the Gulf War, it is likely that Saudi Arabia, weaker militarily than her neighbors, would turn on her Western benefactors.

The same with Iran. When Khatami was elected as president in 1997, many in the West looked on this event as a hopeful turning point in relations with the radical regime in Tehran. However, even Khatami makes anti-Israel statements, even to the Western press.

The fact is, Islam is perpetually traveling the road of war, bloodshed, political unrest, and terrorism.

> Chairman of the Palestinian National Authority Yasser Arafat met here [Tehran] on Thursday afternoon [August 10, 2000] with the current Chairman of the Organization of the Islamic Conference (OIC), President Mohammad Khatami. During the meeting, Arafat presented a report on the second Camp David talks to the Iranian president. Stressing that the issue of Qods [Al Quds, this is the Arab word instead of saying "Jerusalem"] is a serious matter for the Islamic world, President Khatami said that Qods belongs to the whole Islamic world, and the Palestinian nation as representative of world Muslims should keep this holy city. Emphasizing that peace should be fair, President Khatami said justice demands that the whole [of] Palestine be liberated first.[2]

By the "whole [of] Palestine," Khatami once again emphasizes the Islamic call to conquer — not just Jerusalem, the West bank and Gaza, they want all of Israel.

Arafat rose through the ranks of the PLO during the 1960s, eventually claiming to speak for the millions of Palestinians scattered throughout the Middle East. However, no one, to my knowledge, has ever publicly asked him where his family is from.

In other words, if Arafat is portraying himself as a refugee from Palestine, why do we never hear from what part of Palestine he and his family were driven from? This is significant when one considers the carefully crafted image Arafat has presented to the world: a freedom fighter for "his people," the Palestinians. This is not a side issue, but one of supreme importance.

Arafat, driven out of Jordan in 1970, along with various PLO factions he controlled — and who tried many times to assassinate King Hussein — landed in Tunisia. From his base in Tunis, the self-styled leader-in-exile directed terrorist attacks against Israeli and American targets.

When he moved closer, geographically, to his goal of liberating Palestine, he found himself in Beirut, Lebanon, embroiled in a vicious civil war.

Lebanon has long been controlled by outside forces, most notably Syria and Iran. By 1982, Arafat had set up his own "state-within-a-state," launching terrorist raids into northern Israel.

Expelled during Israel's "Operation Peace for Galilee" invasion in 1982, Arafat was forced to flee the country. By the end of the decade, the long process of re-shaping his image was well underway.

In 1994, Arafat was awarded the Nobel Peace Prize, along with Israel's Yitzhak Rabin and Shimon Peres.

His public transformation was complete.

*Poster of Arafat in Bethlehem. Note that he envisions
himself as ruler of all Jerusalem.*

NOTES

1 New Content Copyright © 1999 PBS Online and WGBH/
   FRONTLINE, September 18, 2000, http://www.pbs.org/
   wgbh/pages/frontline/shows/binladen/who/interview.html.

2 New Headlines, August 10, 2000, <http://www.president.ir/
   cronicnews/1379/7905/790520/790520.htm&words=israel&
   color=ff0000>.

CHAPTER SEVEN

BARRICADES
TO PEACE

D rive Carefully! Sharp Curve! Jews 75 Miles an Hour!" — sign posted at a sharp bend in the road near Ludwig-shafen, Germany, in the 1930s.

On my 59th trip to the Middle East, in early 1998, I went with the express purpose of gathering material for this book. In an effort to explain the realities of the Middle East peace process, I focused on the big picture — things the average man and woman can digest in a fast-paced world.

One often finds in life that a revisiting of familiar territory, whether it be a book, play, or vacation spot, can reveal new things with each new look. So it was on my trip, when I visited the Jewish community of Ariel, a sparkling, thriving town in the West Bank.

As we motored down the highway, moments away from Ariel, we came to a bus stop. Pausing for traffic, our party noticed a group of people huddled inside a waist-high concrete structure, a few feet away from the partially enclosed booth.

I leaned forward to ask my driver why those people stood behind concrete. "Terrorists sometimes shoot at them," he replied.

Bus stop in the West Bank.

Passing through the hilly countryside, I kept thinking, *How can you make peace with people who shoot at you at a bus stop?*

It's a very good question — a legitimate question — but one that the general public doesn't know to ask.

The Jews of Israel, traumatized by the Holocaust and weary of a half-century of violence, are motivated to pursue peace. Hated in so many countries for thousands of years, the Jews have no desire to stir up trouble. Think about that. If Yasser Arafat can travel freely in the world, but it is dangerous for any Jew to live in an Islamic country, who is the real obstacle to peace?

This is the reality Israel is dealing with today. Scorned by presidents, journalists, and diplomats who demand acquiescence to Palestinian demands, Israel isn't even safe to catch a bus.

For decades, Israel has been blamed for the lack of peace in the Middle East. The Jews, who were given a virtual desert with which to carve out a nation, have industrialized the region and employed millions — including Arabs. Israel today boasts the region's only democratic system, and has been an invaluable friend to the United States.

And yet, she is considered the chief barricade to peace in a historically explosive corner of the world.

But who is the real barricade to peace?

When Egyptian intellectual Abdul Koddus was profiled in an April 13, 1998, *Time* article, he was portrayed as the very embodiment of Arab sophistication. Urbane, articulate, and principled, Koddus nevertheless revealed a fundamental problem with the Jews of Israel. In describing Koddus' views on a variety of issues, correspondent Scott Macleod wrote:

> He and other relative moderates believe despots should be removed, Israel abolished, and society governed by Islamic law.

Hold it, re-wind the tape.

Koddus is described as a relative moderate who, oh, by the way, thinks Israel should be abolished! Not disliked, not eyed warily, not even boycotted. Abolished!

This is an astonishing admission, displayed for the world to see, given *Time*'s wide distribution. But even more shocking is the matter-of-fact attitude taken by journalists of the Western world. For anti-Israel venom is part of the culture in places like Cairo, Damascus, Tehran, Baghdad, etc., but to casually mention that an entire nation should be abolished shows a gross psychological blind spot.

At the conclusion of the article, Koddus "excused himself and went to pray." But to what god does one pray when hating an entire people?

When Saddam Hussein again defied U.N. weapons

inspectors in early 1998, the United States was forced to consider several options, the scariest of which was military intervention. As the situation deteriorated to the point of conflict, Palestinians demonstrated in the streets of Ramallah, Gaza City, Nablus, and elsewhere. The shouts of "Beloved Saddam, blow up Tel Aviv" were heard from the rooftops of Palestinians in Israel.

Rarely in history has a sovereign nation granted citizenship to people sworn to its destruction. The mind reels at such conspicuous hatred.

When Dr. Haidar Aziz, a sociologist at Al-Kuds University in Jerusalem, was asked about Palestinians chanting death threats to Israel from rooftops, he responded:

> The political situation is pushing people to despair, and this is how they vent their despair. That the peace process is stuck is causing deep anger and frustration. The demonstrations are a manifestation of this pressure.[1]

There we have it. A slow-down of the peace process by Israelis insistent on security is justification for condoning mass murder.

According to a January 15, 1998, *Jerusalem Post* article, Palestinian officials warned that unless there was a breakthrough in negotiations for a further Israeli troop withdrawal from the West Bank, an "explosion" was imminent. The *Post* went on to say that some of the officials warned that a new "intifada" could break out, referring to the holy war waged against Israel, starting in 1987 and lasting years. The intifada was one of the factors in the international decision to hold peace talks in Spain and Norway.

Where Arabs consider an intifada to be a struggle for Palestinian statehood, others define it as the murder of innocent civilians, Jews and Arabs.

THE LAST WAR

Many in the media and Arab world insist that an intifada is simply an ideological struggle.

An October 8, 1997, interview with Hamas leader Rantisi, by Dr. Aaron Lerner of the Independent Media Review and Analysis (IMRA), should send chills up the spine of anyone with optimistic illusions about holy war, Arab-style:

> IMRA: What do you see ultimately happening to the people who moved into Israel? We have the people who came from Europe, Russia, the Arab states.
>
> Rantisi: I will tell you something. I feel that it is justice for us to do with Jews as they did with us.
>
> IMRA: To let them stay?
>
> Rantisi: In the same way that they dispossessed our people. They killed thousands of Palestinians in tens of massacres and they destroyed homes. So I think it is just to do with them as they did with us.

That Arab radicals can publicly declare their intentions to literally murder an entire people is astounding. Though not as astounding as gullible minds insisting that it means something else, something essentially benign.

But the Palestinians and their supporters aren't confining their hatred to the Jews of Israel only. In a December 1996 paper issued by the U.S. House of Representatives Task Force on Terrorism and Unconventional Warfare, this sobering assessment was given:

Approaching the New Cycle of Arab-Israeli Fighting

The succession struggle in Saudi Arabia is peaking. The Abdullah faction is determined to seize power through the eviction of the U.S. from the region, the solution of Saudi Arabia's shortage of cash by accepting more lucrative contracts with East Asia at the expense of the West, and by establishing close relations with the radical states as a guarantee against Islamist subversion. The very close Abdallah-Assad [Syrian dictator Hafez Assad] relations constitute the key to Prince Abdallah's rise to power. These relations have already initiated the bombing of Dahran. Prince Abdallah has already promised Damascus to deliver a comprehensive oil embargo against the West in case of a major crisis with Israel.

Did you catch that? Even the West's so-called Arab "allies" have threatened us with an oil embargo if the United States aids Israel. This is one explanation for U.S. pressure on Israel to turn over land to the Palestinians.

The vise being applied to the neck of the United States and her long-time ally, Israel, is tightened rather overtly by people with whom we try to negotiate. And that brings me to my next bit of startling information.

In the 40 years I've studied the Middle East, I've come to establish many important contacts. One of these people, who shall remain nameless to protect his identity, related the following story.

In late 1990, after Iraq's Saddam Hussein invaded Kuwait, my friend was working as a translator in the prime minister's office in Israel. As he worked at his desk, a superior approached him and asked him to translate a message just intercepted by Israeli intelligence; he was then to destroy the piece of paper it was written on.

Scanning the information, my friend discovered that Egyptian President Hosni Mubarak had entered into an agreement with Saddam. It seems that if Israel were to retaliate against Iraq if attacked (which in fact did happen, with 39 scud missiles raining down on Israeli cities), Egypt would enter into the conflict and side with Iraq.

Do you remember the flap that ensued during the Gulf War, when Israel was "restrained" by U.S. President George Bush and Secretary of State James Baker? The reasoning was that the United States would protect Israel from missile attack. Patriot missile batteries were sent to Israel, and U.S. military and intelligence personnel combed Iraq, looking for scud launchers. Through it all, Israel never moved to fire on Iraq, and this puzzled many people who remember the historically swift Israeli responses to terroristic threats.

Now you know. Had Israel fired on Iraq in self-defense, Egypt would have moved to attack Israel from the south, while Saddam hit from the north and east.

Tellingly, whenever any political event occurred in Israel during the tumultuous days of 1999–2000, Arab spokesmen warned of renewed fighting, even war.

Directly threatening Prime Minister-elect Sharon in early 2001, chief Palestinian negotiator Saeb Erekat warned the incoming government that Sharon's policies could be "a recipe for war."

This kind of constant saber-rattling by Israel's neighbors is the real story behind the Middle East peace process. The horrible punch line is that the United States is also a target. Radical hatred demands the shedding of blood.

That is the real barricade to peace.

DEAD MEN DO TELL TALES

Centuries will go by, but from the ruins of our towns and monuments the hatred of those ultimately responsible will always grow anew. They are the people whom we have to thank for all this: international Jewry and its helpers.[2] (from Adolf Hitler's last will and testament, *The Rise and Fall of the Third Reich*.

I live in the Midwest, in Springfield, Missouri. You might be shocked at the hate groups thriving in our part of the world. They hate Jews and any minority you can name. This mindset festers, and then contaminates, and then all hell breaks loose. It is this same attitude that influences Israel's Arab neighbors.

Were the Christian people of Springfield shocked by the *Winrod Letter*, published by the Reverend Gordon Winrod, pastor of Our Savior's Church in Gainesville, Missouri? The anti-Semitic newsletter arrived in thousands of Springfield homes via an "occupant" blanket mailing. It was indeed representative of the worst kind of anti-Semitic trash that has been infecting our area of Missouri for decades.

If you were shocked or surprised, my question is why? Are you amazed to learn that southwest Missouri and northwest Arkansas are probably second only to Idaho as nesting places for racist and anti-Semitic groups?

All around us, permeating our normally good and loving society are vicious groups like the Ku Klux Klan; White Brotherhood; radical racist militias; neo-nazis; Identity Churches; the Aryan Nation; the Covenant, the Sword and Arm of the Lord; etc. It is time for our good people and churches to wake up and shrug off the demons of unconcern, ignorance, and apathy. It is time to get "stirred up" about these serious problems.

We have just learned of a horrible case of anti-Semitism in which a retired psychiatrist, who happens to be Jewish, is being harassed, cursed, slandered, and ostracized, by "Christians." One "loving" Christian, brought up in this fundamentalist community, has actually threatened to kill him, calling him a "dirty Kike."

This peaceful messianic Jewish psychiatrist came to the Ozarks to retire and write Christian poetry and Christian songs. Now he sits in fear, not knowing what might befall him. A Southern Baptist pastor who was sympathetic toward him lost his position in the church and had to leave the community. Right here in Bible Belt Missouri! Although we are not naming the Jewish doctor nor his tormentors in this book, a detailed report was submitted to the *Springfield News Leader*, our local daily newspaper.

One might wonder how, in Christian America, anti-Semitism can flourish in the name of Jesus Christ, a Jewish teacher who taught us to love everyone, even our enemies? Although I have been an ordained Christian minister since 1956, I must lay the blame at the door of the churches.

Since the third century A.D., large segments of the Church have perpetually taught the doctrines of replacement of and contempt for the Jews. This has strengthened the false notion that the Jews are cursed by God above all other people. This evil notion must be done away with. How sad that these erroneous teachings of the Church prepared the way for Hitler, and gave legitimacy to the Nazi attempt to exterminate the Jews. Following are just a few examples of Christian theological anti-Semitism.

Saint Ambrose, one of the Church fathers, spoke harshly when he said that the Jewish synagogue was "a house of impiety, a receptacle of folly, which God himself has condemned." It is no wonder that his followers then went out and set fire to the local synagogue.

Saint Gregory of Nyssa, in the fourth century, eloquently declared the Jews to be "Slayers of the Lord, murderers of the prophets, adversaries of God, haters of God, men who show contempt for the law, foes of grace, enemies of their father's faith, advocates of the devil, brood of vipers, slanderers, scoffers, men whose minds are in darkness, leaven of the Pharisees, assembly of demons, sinners, wicked men, stoners, and haters of righteousness."

John Crysostom said, "The synagogue is worse than a brothel. . . . the temple of demons . . . and the cavern of devils . . . I hate the synagogue . . . I hate the Jews for the same reason."

There are many opportunities for people to get informed, right here in the Ozarks. Several local churches are very pro-Israel. Many clergy as well as lay people resist anti-Semitism in any form.

In July 1998, Bridges for Peace, a Christian, Jerusalem-based group, sponsored a conference hosted by Cornerstone Church, here in Springfield. One of the speakers was police sergeant Allen Hines (MHP), who spoke on "Neo-Nazism and anti-Semitism in the Ozarks." Allen Hines has been featured on my weekly radio program, "God's Word for Today's World."

My pastor, Rev. Scott Temple (Park Crest Assembly of God), recently brought a powerful series of messages on the need for reconciliation. He often speaks out on behalf of the Jewish people. Other courageous local pastors also speak out in this fashion.

In March 1999, Springfield's Cornerstone Church hosted a conference on prayer and spiritual warfare, attended by delegates from the USA, Africa, the Caribbean, Israel, and Canada. Many of the speakers spoke forthrightly about the growing problems of anti-Semitism, Holocaust denial, and hatred of Israel.

More of these educational and spiritual opportunities are forthcoming. If you would like to be informed of upcoming meetings and activities sponsored by Christians United Against Anti-Semitism and Racism (CUAASR), please contact Dr. David Lewis, P.O. Box 14444, Springfield, MO 65814; fax (417) 882-1135; e-mail address: dalewmin@aol.com. Also, visit my website at:

www.DavidAllenLewis.com.

To the leadership and the congregation of Springfield's Temple Israel and to all Jewish people I wish to say, "You do not stand alone. Whenever the beast of anti-Semitism rears its ugly head, CUAASR and enlightened Christians in our community will stand in solidarity with you to expose and defeat the re-occurring evil of anti-Semitism."

NOTES

1 *Jerusalem Post*, February 13, 1998.
2 William L. Shirer, *The Rise and Fall of the Third Reich* (New York: Simon & Schuster, 1990).

THE ROAD TO JERUSALEM

When Iran conducted amphibious military exercises in 1997, the plan was code-named "Al Quds" or "The Road to Jerusalem." An Iranian general insisted that "these maneuvers do not represent a threat to any nation."[1] The ludicrousness of that statement would be laughable were it not uttered by a representative of a country with a blind hatred of Israel.

One gets the feeling that if the United Nations had decided in 1947 to give the Jews a homeland in Bugtussle, Oklahoma, the Palestinian leadership of today would be demanding half of Bugtussle as a capital.

It is worth noting that Jerusalem as a holy city for the Palestinians is an idea of relatively recent origin. How interesting that at this point in time Jerusalem has become such an obstacle for the entire world, not just the nations neighboring Israel. And as Yasser Arafat has gotten bolder with each concession by the Israelis and their American mediators, the PLO chief ups the ante.

It is a little like the old story of the frog being boiled in a pot. While he sits in the water, he is unaware of the change in temperature until it's too late. So, too, will the Israelis and other westerners find out the true nature of

Arafat's goals, once he is within striking distance of the city that has been holy to the Jews for 3,000 years.

Indeed, within the last year Arafat's rhetoric has included more and more blatant references to Jerusalem as the capital of the Palestinians. Note that he doesn't say anymore that the people he has adopted as his own are owed half of Jerusalem, but rather all of it.

Rachel's Tomb — the scene of heavy fighting during the "new intifada."

Further, his allies in the larger Arab nation back him to the hilt, so to speak. No matter what Israel concedes, it's not enough. Sadly, Israel's chief ally is naively complicit in Arafat's nefarious plans.

Certainly, I want to say for the record that I do support freedom of access to Jerusalem's holy sites to Moslems. Please remember that since 1967, Israel has allowed freedom of worship to all peoples of all faiths. Islamic shrines are there and should be respected. I think, though, that we all have gotten a taste of Palestinian respect for Jewish holy places, such as Joseph's tomb in Nablus, destroyed in the fall of 2000, in the intensity of the new intifada.

Why, of all nations, is Israel treated most frequently by a double standard of judgment? From what seething pit of anti-Semitism do the crooked dealings of the Gentile nations come forth?

The capital of Israel is Jerusalem. Embassies of foreign nations belong in the capital city of the host nation. Yet the United States has its embassy in Tel Aviv. What madness is this? I know of no nation in the world, only Israel, that is treated in this insulting and slanderous manner.

Let's make this really plain and simple. Someday the country of Cuba and the USA might decide to make peace, normalize relations, exchange ambassadors, and open embassies in the respective nations. Havana is the capital of Cuba. That is where we would build our embassy and position our ambassador.

Suppose the president of Cuba said, "I will not recognize Washington D.C. as the U.S. capital. You took that land from the Indians and we Cubans think that Washington should be an internationalized city. We propose to put our Cuban embassy in Portland, Oregon." We would send such an insolent Cuban ambassador packing back to Havana, and wash our hands of the whole thing. There would be no diplomatic relations between the United States and Cuba.

Jerusalem has never, in all of history, been the capital of any nation other than Israel, the Jewish people.

Israel has proven to be a true friend of the USA, our only reliable ally in the Mideast. Israel has the only true democracy in the Mideast. Israel more than any other nation has voted for the interests of the USA in the United Nations. I ask you, why do we treat our true friend in such a way as this?

In March 1995, 93 percent of the U.S. Senate signed a letter sent by New York Senators Alfonse D'Amato (R) and Pat Moynihan (D) to Secretary of State Warren Christopher, stating their belief that the U.S. embassy, currently located in Tel Aviv, should be moved to Jerusalem within the time frame of the peace process, or by 1999.

In April 1995, Sen. Jon Kyl (R-AZ) announced his proposal for new legislation which would provide funding for the U.S. embassy in Israel, only if the administration announced by October that the embassy would relocate to Jerusalem and if the United States recognized Jerusalem as the capital of Israel.

In the following month, Senate Majority Leader and then leading Republican presidential contender Bob Dole (R-KS) introduced the bill in the Senate, where it passed with flying colors. The bill allocated $105 million for site surveys and land acquisition.

A similar bill was offered in the House by Speaker Newt Gingrich, and it passed. Now we ask why the construction is delayed. It will shock you to learn that some American Jews are resisting the embassy project, fearful that it will anger the PLO. Many American Jewish leaders are simply afraid to speak out, for fear of being accused of having dual loyalties. I can understand their frustration and fears. That is why it is so important for you and I, as Christians, with no political agenda, to speak out to our congressmen and senators to hasten the building of the U.S. embassy on the recently acquired land in Jerusalem. Christians must boldly declare themselves on this vital issue and send a message to the enemies of Israel who are still, in spite of all the smoke and mirrors rhetoric, bent on the destruction of all Israel. No one can accuse us of having dual loyalties.

PANDERING?

While some saw Mr. Dole's action as little more than pandering to the Jewish and Evangelical Christian vote before his run for the presidency, it was a hard charge to press against the (then) 53-year-old Mr. Kyl. He is a Presbyterian who had just begun his first six-year term in the Senate from a state which has some 72,000 Jews, only about 1.8 percent of the population.

During his four terms in the House of Representatives, Mr. Kyl earned a reputation in pro-Israel circles as one of Congress' leading advocates of the U.S.-Israel program to develop the Arrow missile. A former member of the House Armed Services Committee, he was an ardent opponent of the Clinton administration's plans to make high-quality satellite technology available to Arab states.

For Mr. Kyl, moving the embassy is long overdue. "It's easy for politicians who support Israel to say, the embassy belongs in Jerusalem. But I have seen so many politicians focus on words, not action. Next year is the 3,000th anniversary of the city since King David moved the capital from Hebron. I thought: *This is the time.*"

SILLY ARGUMENT

He does not think much of the Clinton administration's argument that moving the embassy runs counter to America's policy of not recognizing Israel's sovereignty over the city, and could endanger the Israeli-Palestinian peace process.

"The argument has been raised that now is not the time because it would upset the delicate negotiations. There has hardly been a time, except during a time of war, when Israel has not been involved in delicate negotiations. It seemed to us that while there might be some temporary disruption, it will actually be helpful in the long run," he said.

He maintained that the Palestinians "probably need some realism injected into this, because obviously they have people whom they're trying to please who are hard-liners they can never please."

HELPFUL MOVE

"Ironically, it's somewhat beneficial to them to finally get this out on the table so that they can go back and say, 'Look, there are certain things that we're just not going to be able to get, so stop holding out,' " he said. He added that since Israel has stated its intention to retain sovereignty over all of Jerusalem, "it is not honest for the U.S. to hold out the hope to the Palestinians that they're going to be able to prevent Israel from maintaining control over the city."

Although he has visited Israel three times, he has no immediate plans to return. However, he said, he intends to be in Jerusalem when "the first spade of dirt is turned" for the new embassy.

While the State Department, Clinton administration, and the Rabin government were less than enthusiastic about the Jerusalem bill, many observers saw the legislation as little more than the fulfillment of one of President Clinton's campaign promises. During the 1992 campaign, he promised to move the embassy from Tel Aviv to Jerusalem and to recognize Jerusalem as the state's capital.

After the shock of Mr. Arafat's nose-thumbing of Barak's concessions at Camp David in July 2000, Clinton made noises about moving the U.S. embassy to Jerusalem, but in the end it was only more bait. Arafat didn't budge and the embassy stays put.

MERGE

Now that the legislation has been passed, the U.S. embassy in Tel Aviv will probably be merged with the U.S. consulate in Jerusalem. The consulate in Jerusalem has a notorious reputation among American Jews in Israel, who say it operates mainly to help Arabs and is not very responsive to the needs of Jews living in Jerusalem. American parents living in Israel who want to register their children as Americans have frequently reported that the Jerusalem consulate will not print "Israel" on any documents.

Not surprisingly, Arab Americans did not greet the news of Mr. Kyl's proposed legislation happily. In the Saudi daily paper *Asharq al-Awsat*, Dr. James Zogby, president of the Washington-based Arab-American Institute praised the Clinton administration for "remaining quite firm in its determination to adhere to the terms of the peace process."

Dr. Zogby also had kind words for U.S. Ambassador

to Israel, Martin Indyk who, at his Senate confirmation hearings, delivered a strongly worded rebuke to those who support moving the embassy. "It is the president's feeling — the administration's feeling — that we should do nothing to undermine or preempt those negotiations, that we should wait and let the parties sort out this very sensitive issue before doing anything," he said.

Fairer

Those who support the move say it would be fairer to all parties not to allow the Arabs to harbor any hope that Israel will grant them sovereignty over any part of Jerusalem.

And moving the embassy to Jerusalem is popular not only in Congress, but throughout the country. "The majority of Americans, in every poll, support a united Jerusalem as the capital of Israel and placement of our embassy there," said Richard Hellman, president of the Christians' Israel Public Action Campaign.

The Christian Israel Public Affairs Committee (CIPAC), headed up by Richard Hellman in Washington, D.C., was strongly supportive of Mr. Kyl's legislation, and urged all concerned Americans to call their senators and ask them to co-sponsor the bill to move the embassy to Jerusalem. The response to CIPAC's call to action was heeded by many Christians, and we believe this had a strong affect on our legislators.

Split Jewish Community

Even Dr. Zogby recognized he would have an uphill fight with everyone but Jewish Americans, whom he saw as split on the effort. Fortunately, the bill in favor of Israel was passed. Now is the time to demand action on this matter.

"Those who want to force the issue are quite pleased that their efforts have so far won the support of the Senate. Even leading Republican presidential candidate Bob Dole has signed the letter — a fact which has raised genuine concerns among Moslem and Arab-American Republicans who were supporting his campaign," Zogby wrote.

Dr. Zogby had placed his hopes on the administration's ability to derail Congress. "One might recall that President Reagan faced the same pressure and he, too, resisted despite having promised to support such an embassy move during the 1980 campaign against President Carter," he wrote.

Vatican Interference

Mr. Dole's legislation came on the heels of a press report issued by the Vatican, calling for the diminution or cessation of plans by the state of Israel and world Jewry to celebrate the 3,000th anniversary of Jerusalem as a city.

Responding, Rabbi Fabian Schonfeld, chairman of the Rabbinical Council of America's Interfaith Committee, expressed the RCA's "great alarm" at the report. "The only time during the past 2,000 years that the religious prerogatives of every faith community within the confines of Jerusalem have been respected, has been since the Israeli forces liberated the Old City in 1967. It is only under Israeli rule that members of all other religions have enjoyed

Jerusalem's Old City sees a constant troop presence.

THE LAST WAR

full access to their shrines. This fact has been true even of the Temple Mount, the holiest and most revered location in all Judaism. Nevertheless, Israel sustains access to an Islamic mosque," he said.

In a prepared statement, the RCA called on the Israeli government and people "not to be deterred from implementing all celebratory plans." They also asked the world Jewry "and people of good faith to commemorate this momentous event — the 3,000th anniversary of Jerusalem with the proper religious, educational, and celebratory events signifying a united and unified Jerusalem, the eternal capital of the Jewish people, during the upcoming year."[2]

Beyond all political considerations, I propose that the United States should recognize the uniqueness of Jerusalem by carrying out the plan to build a new U.S. embassy in Jerusalem. One wonders what President George W. Bush will do with this political/religious hot potato. Perhaps he will be the one to move the embassy and thus recognize what Ariel Sharon said in his victory speech on February 6, 2001: that Jerusalem will remain the undivided capital of Israel.

Jerusalem is the only city in the whole world that God ever designated as His own city, a Holy City. Not Rome, not New York, nor Chicago, Paris, Geneva, Brussels — *only Jerusalem is the Holy City,* God's special bit of real estate.

WHEN NEGOTIATIONS HIT THE WALL

The Palestinian National Authority (PNA) in 1997 threatened to escalate terrorist attacks on Israel unless then-Prime Minister Netanyahu stopped the construction on the *Har Homa* (the Hill of the Wall, in Hebrew) site in Jerusalem. Some PNA and Hamas spokespersons threatened all-out war based on the same complaint.

The whole Har Homa controversy originates from misinformation, deliberate deception and incitement by the Palestinians, the media, and certain left-wing Israelis. Naturally, their hostile alliance soon grew to include anti-Israel groups in America, Europe, and Arab countries.

The knee jerk, anti-Israel reaction of the secular media has produced outright lies about the Har Homa project. Lies like "Israel is bulldozing Arab homes to clear space for building new Jewish apartments," and "There are riots in the streets of Har Homa!"

Several people told me then about TV news reports showing the Har Homa riots, the rioting of Palestinians protesting the Israeli building project. At least one of these false reports even showed what was alleged to be video film of the riots in the streets of Har Homa. Palestinians and Israeli troops were shown locked in combat. Rocks were thrown and guns fired. This blatant deception became apparent when Tom Brimmer and I went to Har Homa. There is no town or village of Har Homa. Where then did the video film come from? Our investigation indicates that the footage was taken of a riot in Gaza, months earlier!

We have a European "insider" intelligence report in our hands which confidently declares, "With bulldozers leveling Palestinian homes and clearing ground for settlements in East Jerusalem, tension in the world's most explosive areas was nearing breaking point. At that moment, it would seem that the Israeli prime minister made matters worse by declaring, 'I am building Har Homa (the settlement for 32,000 more people in the occupied

Har Homa

West Bank) and nothing is going to stop me.' "

This statement is false as we will demonstrate. Netanyahu had not said any such thing.

WE SAW HAR HOMA

Tom and I did more than conduct interviews and read documents. We went to the site and took over 50 photographs. It is a partly forested hill and there are no houses, let alone an Arab village there.

No buildings have been destroyed. There were never any homes or buildings on Har Homa. There are some Arab villages nearby, and they have not been disturbed. The planned neighborhood is to be built on an unpopulated area near a Jewish kibbutz, Ramat Rachel, within the municipal boundaries of the city of Jerusalem.

JERUSALEM IS GROWING

Jerusalem is a vibrant, growing city. The purpose of the Har Homa project is to alleviate the housing shortage for both the Jewish and Arab residents of the city. As such, it constitutes part of the overall municipal plan (not just Har Homa) to construct 20,000 new housing units for the Jewish sector and 8,500 for the Arab sector — a ratio comparable to that of the Jewish and Arab populations in the city.

With Jews of all different appearances, even Ethiopians,

Har Homa

coming to Israel, the need for land and housing is apparent. One can hear the questions birthed by Isaiah being asked today:

> For thy waste and thy desolate places, and the land of thy destruction, shall even now be too narrow by reason of the inhabitants, and they that swallowed thee up shall be far away. The children which thou shalt have, after thou hast lost the other, shall say again in thine ears, The place is too strait for me: give place to me that I may dwell. Then shalt thou say in thine heart, Who hath begotten me these, seeing I have lost my children, and am desolate, a captive, and removing to and fro? and who hath brought up these? Behold, I was left alone; these, where had they been? (Isa. 49:19–21).

In this regard, consider what Netanyahu said in 1997: "We will build in Jerusalem, without conditions, without restrictions. We will build throughout the city . . . we are as committed to the Arab residents of Jerusalem as we are to providing for the Jewish residents. They, too, need housing, and we will build, adapting the building plans to the needs of both populations."

At Har Homa, an area of 1,850 *dunams* of land (about 460 acres) was expropriated by the Israeli government for the Har Homa project. Of this, 1,400 dunams came from Jewish owners and 450 dunams from Arab owners. Among the parcels expropriated, the largest (almost 800 dunams, or about 43 percent) belonged to David Meeri, who is Jewish.

Much of the 1,400 dunams owned by Jews was purchased prior to 1948. Following the 1948 War of Independence, in which Jordan occupied the West Bank and half of Jerusalem, the Jordanian Custodian of Enemy Property planted a pine forest at Har Homa to prevent misuse of the land by local Jordanian residents. Since East Jerusalem was liberated in the Six Day War, that forest has been maintained by the Jewish National Fund.

VACANT LOTS

All of this land in question is vacant, most of it forested. No homeowner, Jewish or Arab, will be displaced by the project. All owners were offered full compensation for the land taken. Nevertheless, both the Arab and Jewish owners contested the expropriation in court.

The matter eventually reached the High Court, which denied the claims and ruled in favor of the government. The High Court of Justice upheld the government's right to appropriate this land in order to meet the housing needs of the public at large.

NO BASIS FOR PNA CLAIMS

There is no basis to the Palestinian claims that the planning construction constitutes a violation of the agreements between Israel and the Palestinians. These agreements do not place any restrictions on Israeli building in areas under Israeli control. Read it for yourself in the agreements. That Israel violates the agreements is one of the neatly packaged lies propagated by her enemies.

Both the Declaration of Principles (1993) and the Interim Agreement (1995) state that the issue of Jerusalem will be discussed in the framework of the permanent status negotiations, and that the Palestinian side has no authority in Jerusalem during the interim period. Under these agreements, the Palestinians have no standing to demand that Israel coordinate building in Jerusalem with them.

Far from being a right-wing scheme to cheat the Arabs, the Har Homa project was undertaken by the previous Labor-led administration. Many members of parliament, aligned with centrist parties, are in favor of continued building in the city of Jerusalem, the capital of Israel. What started out as a standard building project for another suburb com-

munity of Jerusalem has become a test case of might between the PNA and Israel, vis-a-vis the future of Jerusalem and the negotiations for the "final status" of the city.

The Knesset (parliament) has stated repeatedly that Jerusalem is not up for discussion and it will remain the undivided capital of the state of Israel and the Jewish people. Now, PLO officials have stated that any attempt to build on Har Homa in particular, or in Jerusalem in general, will be deemed a violation of the accords and a "declaration of war."

Knesset members who are calling themselves the "Land of Israel Front" are forging ahead to pressure the government to give the okay for the project and its immediate beginning. Jerusalem Mayor Ehud Olmert stated that the Har Homa project is the final straw regarding what he sees as unfavorable governmental policies regarding building in the capital. Olmert made clear he would not tolerate a postponement of the scheduled building.

This whole *balagan gadol* (big chaos) is not about Har Homa. It is about continuing the pressure applied to Israel, which is paving the "Road to Jerusalem" for the enemies of the Jewish state. Actually, Har Homa may seem to be a moot consideration in the light of the current battles going on in Jerusalem. However, Har Homa looms on the horizon and will ultimately have to be dealt with.

TEMPLE TURMOIL IN THE OLD CITY

In 1969 I crawled on my hands and knees into a low opening that led to a huge vaulted hall under the Street of Chains. The Six Day War of 1967 had given Israelis access to this historical treasure.

Later, Dan Bahat led one of our groups to the end of the tunnel and back, giving the best lecture I have heard on the subject. Following is a summary of information from some reliable sources. Much of this background report is from the September 25, 1996, issue of the Israeli newspaper *Ha'aretz*, and was written by Nadav Shragai. The following is largely a translation from Hebrew.

The Hasmonean Tunnel, opened at the foot of the perimeter of the Temple Mount, served as an aqueduct in the Hasmonean Period, and was already discovered in the previous century by the explorers Charles Wilson and Konrad Schick. Until 13 years ago, and for more than 100 years, no one had entered it; it remained forgotten in the depths of the earth, full of mud and water, under houses in the Moslem Quarter [of the Old City of Jerusalem].

It was only in 1987 that the Ministry for Religious Affairs re-excavated the tunnel and connected it to the Western Wall tunnel, another tunnel about 500 meters long, exposing the Western Wall along its entire length. The work was carried out at the time by archeologist Dan Bahat, and there was great excitement at the renewed discovery.

The length of the Hasmonean Tunnel is about 80 meters, [86.6 yards] its height seven

The Western Wall, with the Temple Mount above, at the tree line.

meters [7.58 yards], its width a little less than one meter [39 in.]. It closes in on those walking through as in a narrow canyon. At the time, archeologists said it was equal in importance to the Shiloah (Siloam) Pool. Originally, the tunnel was dug as a water aqueduct, an open channel on a hillside. The portion connected to the Western Wall tunnel is the southern segment of a much longer aqueduct, which emerged from north of the city near the Damascus Gate; there, it apparently drained the flood waters of the Tyropian stream, across from the Temple Mount.

At its northern end, it joined up with the southern part of a small pool, cut across its middle by a wall, the Starothyon Pool, under the monastery [sic. convent] of the Sisters of Zion (Soeurs de Sion). The nuns there built the dividing wall to block access to explorers and archeologists in the previous century, for fear that strangers would try to penetrate into the monastery [sic. convent] through the part of the pool in its grounds. The Roman emperor Adrian [Hadrian] had also divided the Starothyon Pool, in another direction, lengthwise.

For several years, employees of the Ministry for Religious Affairs and the Corporation for the Development of East Jerusalem engaged in cleaning out the tunnel and the part of the pool which had not been demarcated by the Sisters of Zion.

In the nine years since the link-up between the two tunnels (that of the Western Wall, and the Hasmonean), the Wakf [the Moslem religious authority] succeeded in foiling a number of plans meant to permit movement of tourists and hikers from the Wall Plaza, through the Western Wall Tunnel and the Hasmonean Tunnel, up to ground level, in the markets of the Old City. The Religious Affairs Ministry tried several times to open up an entrance from the end of the Hasmonean Tunnel up to ground level, near the Temple Mount (but not actually within it).

Time after time, the Wakf and the Supreme Moslem Council set off disturbances, and the plans were disrupted, until they were frozen for some years by the decision of the security authorities. Three years ago, it was decided to dig a passage for pedestrians, a short additional tunnel, with steps, for a stretch of about 15 meters, from the Starothyon Pool up to the vicinity of the stairway leading to the Al-Omariya School.

That work was completed a year and a half ago: the directorate of the Wall, the Jerusalem Municipality, the Religious Affairs Ministry and the East Jerusalem Development Corporation waited for a "green light" from the political echelon to carry out the final breakthrough.

At the conclusion of Yom Kippur 1996, approval was granted, and within an hour-and-a-half the entrance was broken open.

TEMPLE TERROR

On September 27, 1996, under the direction of the Netanyahu government, Israel made an opening at the end of the 2,000-year-old tunnel near the Temple Mount, in Jerusalem. The tunnel is toured by thousands each year, and the bottleneck created as people go through forces delays as tourists turn and make their way back. To facilitate a free-flowing traffic, the opening was made.

Immediately, Yasser Arafat and his spokesmen cried that Israel was burrowing under Islamic shrines (the Dome of the Rock, and the Al-Aqsa mosque, both on the Temple Mount). Although this was absolutely false, Arafat's incitement triggered bloody clashes between Palestinians and Israelis. Within one week, 70 people lay dead.

Indeed, the media reported that the tunnel in question ran underneath the Al-Aqsa Mosque. This is blatantly untrue, but how many people can travel to Jerusalem and see for themselves?

The tunnel opening didn't disturb any sites, religious or otherwise, but the propaganda effect for the Palestinians was worth more than any Madison Avenue ad agency could provide. To this day, the incident is still used to portray Israel as a fiendish destroyer of Islamic holy sites.

Ironically — and almost totally unreported by the world media — the new tunnel doorway opens onto the Via Dolorosa, in the Arab section of the Old City. This allows tourists to walk directly into Arab shops and spend money.

A further insight into this mindset of bias occurred during my February 1998 visit to Israel. One cool, rainy morning, a group of my friends were treated to a rare viewing of "Solomon's Stables," a Herodian-era architectural marvel located on the Temple Mount, directly underneath the Al-Aqsa Mosque.

Jerusalem's Temple Mount, today dominated by the Dome of the Rock (left) and the Al-Aqsa Mosque (dome at right).

THE LAST WAR

Shoeless, the group was taken on a tour (with only Moslem tour guides, since Jews are forbidden on the Temple Mount) through the catacombs. The musty, stone passageways led this way and that. Stopping at a place exhibiting Roman and Byzantine architecture, the tour guide pointed to an arched doorway located behind an iron gate.

As the tour guide explained the history of the place, he informed the group that tradition says the prophet Mohammed entered the mosque through this particular doorway. Failing to realize that Mohammed couldn't very well enter a mosque *before* he founded the religion of Islam,

Excavated ruins — Old City of Jerusalem.

the guide continued sanitizing any history other than that of Islam. In other words, he never mentioned the Jewish, Roman, or Byzantine connection to these sites.

In fact, the Al-Aqsa Mosque was originally a Byzantine church. But to Arabs, it was never anything but a holy Islamic shrine. Sadly, Palestinian people are force-fed revisionist history, perpetuating falsehoods that deny mutual respect for Jewish neighbors.

The puzzle of Jerusalem remains jumbled. I have never talked to any of my numerous Middle East contacts — Jews and Arabs — who seem to have a workable solution to the controversial claims.

By early 2001, everyone from Ariel Sharon to committed peace doves were speculating that the issue of Jerusalem might be shelved for far-future generations.

EHUD OLMERT INTERVIEW

Ehud Olmert, a member of the Knesset since 1973 and a key Likud Party figure, met with us at his office in downtown Jerusalem. As mayor of the most contentious city in the world, his time was valuable, so we were all the more grateful that he took the time to share with us his thoughts about Jerusalem.

Meeting with us was my son-in-law, Neil Howell.

In late 2000, as a final push was made for a peace treaty between the Israelis and Palestinians, and when it became clear that Ehud Barak was willing to give up control of the Temple Mount, Olmert moved his offices temporarily to the Western Wall plaza in a solidarity move aimed at uniting the Jews of Israel.

David Lewis: We are going to talk to you about the truth about the situation in Jerusalem. I would like to present you with a copy of my book, *Can Israel Survive in a Hostile World?*

Ehud Olmert: Thank you very much.

David Lewis: I am writing another volume. It will be a sequel to this book. It will deal in part about the misrepresentation of Israel in the media. First of all, we are not surprised when the Western media bashes Israel, when they treat Israel badly. There is a lot of latent anti-Semitism in the world, and we feel that it is in part a manifestation of that anti-Semitism.

Ehud Olmert

It's not polite to be anti-Semitic anymore, but you can be anti-Israel or anti-Zionist and have a respectable. . . .

Ehud Olmert: Compensate your anti-Semitic feelings being anti-Israeli.

David Lewis: So, we find that what the press says about

Israel in the media and television and radio in America is usually off center, if not an absolute lie. And I would like to ask you this question: Why do you think the Western media is so universally against Israel? What's the purpose behind this?

Ehud Olmert: Well, I think basically I don't have any better answer than you have, which is that there is a mixture of, number one, the fundamental anti-Semitic attitude which is characteristic of some of those countries. You know, I always say that to believe that these monstrous movements that try to annihilate the whole Jewish world, that suddenly all this has disappeared since the Second World War — I mean, this is ridiculous. Of course it's there and it's there in a very substantial way and has its impact on their relations with us. That's number one. Number two, I think that there is a perception that the conflict in the Middle East has changed. Until 1967 the perception was that Israel is facing the whole Arab world and therefore we are the good guys because we are the victims and we are the small and weak side and they are the powerful, threatening aggressor. And the world tends to identify with the underdog, so to say. Since 1967 gradually this perception has changed and from being the underdogs we became the aggressors and the Palestinians became the underdogs and it became fashionable to identify with the Palestinians as the victim and not as the aggressor. And I think that that has contributed to the status of the Palestinians relative to ours in the public opinion.

David Lewis: I could understand, as I said earlier, that the Western media is anti-Israel, but it's rather shocking to come back here this time and study the media in Israel and find out that they are losing their Zionist values.

Ehud Olmert: Well, this is a long process. It hasn't started in the last couple of years. It's been long ago. We suffer from the same syndrome as some of your societies. The European Union, the Americans, many of them disagree with Israel on the Israeli-Arab conflict; they disagree with themselves, and within themselves, and amongst themselves about many other issues regarding their relations with underdeveloped countries. Almost automatically in any such conflict, the Western society is guilty of something in the mind of many of the policymakers of those countries. And this is the same syndrome of self-hating, of being held responsible for all the malaise and all the vices of the others. And I think it reflects itself partly in their attitude toward the state of Israel, but it goes beyond there. I think the same happens within Israel amongst many different factions. You hear some of the historians, they're what we call now the post-Zionist historians. . . .

David Lewis: Revisionists.

Ehud Olmert: The new historians, you know, who describe the battle for the Jewish people, of the Jewish people for independence in the state of Israel as, in terms of aggression and colonialism and you know, it's unbelievable. It happens, but I say this kind of garbage, this kind of distortion can't prevail. The truth will be stronger and it will prevail. The true historical account will prevail. The other day, General Barak, former chief of staff and our leader of the Labor Party said that when asked whether he could imagine himself being a Palestinian, a young Palestinian, what would he do? He said, "Obviously if I'd been a young Palestinian I would have joined the terrorist organizations, and so on and so forth. I was asked today on TV to comment on this. And I said first of all, I can't envision myself a Palestinian, it's not a technical thing. I don't identify. I envision myself exactly what I am — a Jew living in his own country and that's it. And I say don't try and trap me, because I will not be trapped."

The worst part in what Barak said is that he tried to allude to the historical debate about the nature of what has been the Jewish underground movement that fought here against the British. Basically what he wanted to say, which is a full distortion of the true historical account, is that as the Israelis were terrorists against the British, so the Palestinians are entitled to be terrorists against us. This is a fundamental distortion of Jewish history. We never had terrorist organizations in Israel. We had underground movement. We never made it into a system to kill innocent civilians. We may have killed some, unfortunately. We always regretted it and we always tried to avoid it. And what they're doing as a matter of system, as a matter of policy, they're killing innocent people because they are terrorists. So how can one draw a conclusion on the basis of what they do to us ourselves? This is a total distortion of the reality and the background of history. And unfortunately it happens, but we are strong enough to overcome this.

And I'm not certain that the Israeli press is so influential. Had it been so influential, Bibi [Netanyahu's childhood nickname, but still widely used] wouldn't have been elected prime minister. I would have never been elected mayor of Jerusalem. Thank God. They write and we do.

Ben Yehuda Street, downtown Jerusalem. The scene of terrorist bombings.

David Lewis: That's good. In America, the press and the media have given the impression that the Har Homa housing project is displacing Arabs from their ancient homes. Now we've been out to Har Homa, we see what's there, we see what's not there, and what is in the press is an absolute distortion. Why, even one reporter said there was fighting in the streets of Har Homa, rioting in the streets of Har Homa. We didn't see any people living there. We didn't see houses. In fact we didn't even see any streets. All we saw was a tree-covered hill.

Ehud Olmert: Look, Har Homa is not a settlement to start with. The use of the term "settlement," widely done by the international community, is already an attempt to establish a certain connotation. Settlement . . . unfortunately, as it turned out in the last few years, has become synonymous with occupation. You say settlement, you mean occupation. They try. They call it a settlement. Why is this a settlement? This is a housing project in the middle of Jerusalem, just like any other housing project in the middle of Berlin, in the middle of Frankfurt, in the middle of London, in the middle of Moscow. And I resent the attempt to call it a settlement. This is not a settlement. This is a housing project. There were three or four hundred different owners for this plot. We tried to work out a city plan that would be accepted by all, but it became virtually impossible for all the different owners of plots in this big parcel of land to agree on a particular city plan. So the only way to do it was to expropriate this land from its owners, to pay them a compensation and a very high compensation, and to build it as one unit, and that's what we plan to do. Now those who appealed against us were not Arabs, because they hardly own anything there. Those who appealed against us in court were Jews because they are the owners of most of the land there in the first place. So number one, it's in the middle of town; number two, it was expropriated from Jews. Where exactly is the violation on the rights of the Palestinians here? I don't know. But again, who cares for the facts? Who cares for the true account of what happens? Everyone cares to say how desperate the Palestinians are, how much they sympathize with the Palestinians, the Palestinians are victims of the aggression of the Jewish government in Jerusalem, and so forth. And there are, I hope, enough people in America and in other communities that understand the nonsense of this argument and these descriptions.

David Lewis: That is how we feel that this book is going to be helpful.

Ehud Olmert: We hope so.

David Lewis: Let's talk about Gershon Salomon [leader of the Temple Mount Faithful Movement] and the1990 riot on the Temple Mount. How did they [Palestinians] get all those rocks up there? If this was supposed to be a spontaneous riot on the part of the Arabs, what were they all doing up there in the first place? I've gone to the Temple Mount and I don't see loose rocks laying around.

Ehud Olmert: Obviously there was no spontaneity there.

David Lewis: Well planned.

Ehud Olmert: It was well planned according to the account that we have found.

David Lewis: What is Gershon trying to do?

Ehud Olmert: Look, Gershon is trying to do something which I personally can sympathize with, but I agree with government policy that says let's not stretch ourselves beyond certain borders. Gershon Salomon wants, as a Jew, to have a right to pray in the most sacred place for Jewish history, that's all. That's very simple and very natural and very understandable. The government policy says look, it's definitely right, it's definitely justified, it's just going to ignite such a confrontation that perhaps it will be better off for all of us to avoid it for the time being even though you are basically right in your demand to exercise your religious right and pray on the Temple Mount. This is the most sacred, the most important, the most sensitive place in the universe and this is ours and it's tied up to our history. It's tied up to our religion. How can anyone deny Jews from praying there? So it's a very understandable demand. Yet, as I said, the outcome of exercising your right may erupt in terrible hostilities, so you know, you should impose on yourself a certain restriction for a period of time. I've known him for many years, talked to him many times. He has a cornerstone for the temple which he tries every Succoth to get up on the Mount. He knows in advance that it is going to be stopped. I think that to him it is symbolic of the Jewish desire for the third temple and for the mountain, the place of sacred prayer.

Jim Fletcher: In America, we're fed a steady diet of the phrase *Arab* East Jerusalem. What does that mean and where did the term come from?

Ehud Olmert: This is a part of the violation and distortion perpetrated by those who want to split the city and to create a new political agenda for Jerusalem, but it's ridiculous. When was Jerusalem ever Palestinian? When was it ever other than Jewish? What else was it ever in history in the last 3,000 years? It never was a capital for Palestinians. The Palestinian people did not exist a hundred years ago. With all due respect, this is a new phenomenon. I don't want to argue now what is the validity of this phenomenon — whether we should recognize it or not; it's a different issue, but it's a new phenomenon. A hundred years ago there were no Palestinian people, or else I'm completely ignorant. You can't take one book, one book with a hard cover or with a soft cover, that will use the term "the Palestinian people" a hundred years ago. It's a new phenomenon that started only in this century. When was it the sovereign in Jerusalem? When was Islam or any Muslim country ever making Jerusalem their capital? Never. They never made Jerusalem into the capital. It never was their capital.

The last 178 years Jerusalem has a consistent Jewish majority. So to call me the mayor of West Jerusalem and Fisal Husseini or whoever the mayor of East Jerusalem — this is a ridiculous violation of the law. But what can I do? I think that more people from the east side of Jerusalem accept me as the mayor of all of the city than they accept Fisal Huseini as mayor of part of the city. That's all.

NOTES

1 "In the News," *Arkansas Democrat-Gazette*, June 8, 1997.
2 *The Jewish Voice*, June 1995.

CHAPTER NINE

THE
LAST WAR

On the December 27, 2000, broadcast of NBC's "Tonight Show," host Jay Leno laughed his way through a segment in which he asked people on the street a series of questions, to test their knowledge. The first question required the respondents to name the two groups in the Middle East who are negotiating a historic peace treaty.

The first person answered, "China and Russia."

The second thought for several seconds before replying, "Saudi Arabia and Japan."

The third person answered "Iran and Iraq," so Leno decided to give a few clues. He informed his subject that one was a Jewish state.

"Jerusalem?"

That Jerusalem is not a country compelled the late-night comedian to laugh some more, as he highlighted the fact that several of the countries given as answers are not even on the right continent.

As the saying goes, it would have been funny if it weren't so tragic.

When William B. Oden traveled with an ecumenical church delegation to the Holy Land in December 2000, the president of the Council of Bishops of the United Methodist

Church came home outraged over what he described to reporter Diane Huie Balay as "the extent to which Palestinians are suffering violence and injustice from Israelis." The delegation had even talked with a seemingly distressed Yasser Arafat, who told the group that "we are facing disaster," a reference to what he said were Israeli provocations.

Articles about the visit were published in many Christian newspapers, and were widely distributed by such church media organizations as the United Methodist News Service, representing 8.4 million United Methodists (the second-largest Protestant denomination in the United States, behind the Southern Baptists).

That type of media coverage cloned the PLO message for dissemination to millions of Americans, many of whom find themselves each Sunday in a mainline church (Presbyterian, United Methodist, Episcopalian, Lutheran, etc.). Routinely, this kind of distributed information is wholly lacking in the opposing viewpoint, such as when writers and other observers lament the destruction of Palestinian homes from Israeli shelling. The reader is never told why the shelling is taking place, nor is he apprised of the fact that over the course of the latest intifada, the Israeli forces could have inflicted thousands of deaths on Palestinians, not hundreds.

Thus, Israel finds itself fighting an information war on several fronts. There is both widespread ignorance of the issues, and bias. Many of my Israeli friends, competent and experienced journalists among them, are at a loss to come up with an effective strategy.

Regarding the Middle East, Americans are either apathetic, ignorant of basic facts, or brainwashed by media bias.

Not surprisingly, many Israelis are unaware of the roots of this war, this last war. In this, they can even join Americans. From the time of Charles Darwin's invasion of the Book of Genesis in the mid-19th century (preceded somewhat by the philosophical writings of men like Baruch

THE LAST WAR

Spinoza and Jean Astruc), the ground was being prepared for a strange harvest. This crop would feed a world view that to this day has a distorted sense of history and has a direct bearing on the Middle East.

Once Genesis had been mythologized in the minds of millions of churchgoers, through seminary professors who in turn produced generations of Western clergy, the door was opened for an assault on the Jews' right to claim the Holy Land. The Hebrew Bible, what Christians call the Old Testament, was no longer God's message spoken through a succession of Jewish prophets, it was now a dreamlike novel of symbolism, legend, and outright fabrication.

Suddenly, prophecies concerning the regathering of the scattered Jews into the land promised by God to Abraham were merely a historical anamoly. It is possibly the only paradigm shift in history that is, for all practical purposes, invisible to humanity.

How did this come about and, more importantly, why is it critical to us?

Many people have the idea that the prophecies found in books like Ezekiel, Isaiah, Jeremiah, Zechariah, and Amos, among a dozen others, are either symbolic or worse, vague.

For those who take the time to actually read the Old Testament, without the biased glasses of liberal scholarship, it can be clearly demonstrated that the return of the Jews to the land between the Mediterranean and the Jordan River was foretold even before the exile to Babylon in 586 B.C.!

Sadly, most Christians neither understand nor care about that and yet it so directly affects their lives.

Take, for example, God's amazing dialogue in the first three verses of Zechariah 12:

> The burden of the word of the Lord for Is-
> rael, saith the Lord, which stretcheth forth the
> heavens, and layeth the foundation of the earth,
> and formeth the spirit of man within him. Behold,

> I will make Jerusalem a cup of trembling unto all the people round about, when they shall be in the seige both against Judah and against Jerusalem. And in that day will I make Jerusalem a burdensome stone for all people: all that burden themselves with it shall be cut in pieces, though all the people of the earth be gathered together against it.

To the liberal Christian mind, these verses merely mean that the enemies of God from time to time attack those who follow Him. For them, it has nothing to do with a historical future war between the Jewish state and the nations of the world.

Likewise, the famous "dry bones" prophecy from Ezekiel 37 reflects the restoration of dead, dry churches to right fellowship with God, according to this narcissistic view of the Gentile church. This is almost universally taught in American pulpits, including the Pentecostal and Baptist churches, long considered to be Israel's greatest friends.

However, in the 11th verse, God himself identifies the passage as referring to "the house of Israel." The chapter indicates that the Jewish people will one day return to the land promised to Abraham, Isaac, and Jacob, then return to worshiping the one true God.

In large part because these kinds of passages are taught symbolically, American discernment has been dulled with regard to present-day Middle East realities.

Israeli political observer Ya'akov Kirschen (of "Dry Bones" cartoon fame) sat with us in a Tel Aviv café one spring evening in 1998 and marveled at the widespread ignorance concerning Bible prophecies. He related a fascinating insight, telling us that when he was growing up in the 1940s, God's demise was actually a popular dinner topic.

"But then the Jews came back to Israel, and you would have thought that people all over the world would have said, 'My God, it's happened,' and fallen down on their knees to worship the God of the Bible. But they didn't."

Ya'akov went on to add some more detail. "Before 1948, whenever a crazy Christian preacher or a Jewish rabbi would predict that one day the Jewish people would be re-gathered into their land, people would pat them on the head and say, 'Sure, sure.' But then it happened! Instead of amazement, there was all of a sudden a lot of anger. People became angry."

All through the prophetic Scriptures, the dominant theme is Jewish spiritual rebellion against God, followed by punishment and exile, followed finally by return and restoration. Indeed, there are numerous passages which warn the nations of the world about plotting against the Jews (see Jer. 30; Isa. 49; Ps. 83).

As far back as Deuteronomy (chapter 30), when the children of Israel under Moses were baking in their desert exile, God presented the sweep of Jewish history and destiny.

The teaching that has permeated American churches and, thus, the American media representatives, politicians, and cultural commentators, has been something quite different. For them, the Bible is an outdated collection of human writings rife with weird imagery and nationalistic fiction.

> The second section [of Genesis], chapters 12 through 50, is made up of hero stories out of the semi-legendary past of the Hebrew people.[1] (*Beyond the Point of No Return*, Calvin B. Johnson, quoting Methodist literature from the 1950s).

This was the educational background of Bishop Oden, the aforementioned traveler to the Holy Land, and many, many others like him. To them, Israel's divine right to the land is simply not there.

Therefore, seeing the Palestinian Arabs as helpless victims of Israeli brutality, legions of cultural Christians in the West have abandoned any thought that the Jews are the true heirs of Israel, or Palestine, or the Holy Land, or whatever one wants to call it.

The world view that says God promised the land to the Jews forever, and is preparing to intervene again in human history is so absurd to most minds that it belongs in the realm of crackpot theories.

Worst of all, while Christian fundamentalists and other conservatives are labeled as anti-intellectual by enlightened scholars, those same educators are completely closed off to dialogue about the subject. The intolerance of the self-styled tolerant is something to behold.

While compiling research for this book, we contacted several well-known Christian leaders from mainline backgrounds. During one phone conversation, a member of the clergy said, "One cannot find Israel's fate in the Bible."

This statement, so typical of the truly influential churches in America, is so blatantly wrong, one struggles to find words of rebuttal.

To repeat, a non-symbolic reading of Scripture would lead a reader to conclude that God is preparing to rise from His dwelling place and shake off the mockings of His creation, specifically to usher in an era of true global peace. This idea, again, is patently absurd to the very people it warns.

It is popular for pro-Palestinian Westerners to poohpooh the idea that the Bible exclusively awards the Holy Land to the Jews, claiming that the Arabs, too, are children of Father Abraham, that Semitic nomad who crossed the Fertile Crescent on orders of the deity, probably around 1750 B.C.

Certainly, they are half right: the Arabs are brothers/cousins of the Jews, tracing their lineage from Abraham's first-born son, Ishmael. However, in Genesis 21, in successive verses (12 and 13), God explains to Abraham that "in Isaac shall thy seed be called," and that of Ishmael would He also "make a nation."

Isaac was "the child of the promise," and, in fact, his

son Jacob was renamed Israel by God, to signify a special relationship with a nation of people called to be "a light unto the nations." That is, the Jews were to proclaim the truth of a personal and all-powerful God to the world.

Unfortunately, many Christian institutions have skewed this truth about Israel and the Jews, reducing them to just another physically and spiritually evolving people.

In his remarkable book *Controversy of Zion*, Claude Duvernoy mused about this distorted view of history:

> But who among the powerful and wise reads Isaiah? They only read their own specialized reports, their scientific literature and, in addition and for their recreation, as they say, works of science fiction, crime stories or simply the horoscopes in their morning paper. They read everything, they know everything, these poor men, everything except Isaiah![2]

John Shelby Spong, the recently retired Episcopal bishop of New Jersey, is among the leading proponents of the symbolic/mythical/legendary view of the Bible. Encountering graduate students early in his career, Spong, who apparently abandoned any "literalist" leanings early on, had this to say about those who view the Bible as an inspired communication from God:

> A few of their number had chosen to become anti-intellectual and to cling to their religious traditions in the face of all the odds. They became the religious fanatics of the campus who revealed anxiety, fear, and vulnerability beneath their closed minds and deep religious anger.[3]

One wonders how Spong can discern such massive religious anger, but there is no doubt that he views Bible literalists as deluded and possibly dangerous. The "security seekers" in "the unthinking churches" are presumably the ones Spong believes have not been enlightened in the new theology. This new theology, of course, seeks first to destroy the historicity of Genesis, then fictionalize the great prophetic themes of exile and restoration as they apply to the Jewish people. This type of thinking has clouded our perceptions regarding Israel's right to the biblical land.

Because many "prophecies" found in the ancient Sumerian writings (such as Akkadian texts) were written after the fact, it is presumed by certain influential scholars that Bible prophecies were also written after the fact, rendering them, of course, worthless in terms of future realities.

It is for this reason that liberal scholars of the past hundred years have worked mightily to assign multiple authors for the Bible's prophetic books, so that the wondrous predictions for the Jews to be restored to their land "in the last days" are really nothing more than works of fiction designed to boost the faith of Jews in distressing circumstances (Babylonian captivity, Roman exile, etc.).

All of a sudden, Isaiah wasn't recording God's plan for the future, he was really an anonymous collection of Hebrew scribes writing after the fact.

The significance of this new Bible analysis is that the Church, and by extension, secular society, no longer can discern the wonderful promises found in the Bible, first for the Jewish people and then for all of mankind.

The truly stunning aspect of all this is that as the Bible prophecies grow more pregnant, the world is paying less and less attention, preferring to believe that Bible prophecy is represented by the views of fanatics.

In fact, it is Zechariah who is most relevant. Remember the references to Jerusalem being a cup of trembling and a burdensome stone?

What if they're not symbolic?

What if they mean exactly what they say? If they refer

to a future time, in which the nations of the world will be judged according to their treatment of Israel, what does that say for us today? Look at a list of U.N. countries that support a Palestinian state. They would be better served to list the countries that don't, for it would be a short list indeed.

Why can the world not see the plain message of Zechariah when the Israeli foreign minister regularly meets with his counterparts from Spain, France, China, South Africa, the United States, Germany, England, and Russia? Why are all these nations involved in the territorial disputes involving ancient cousins?

Dave Hunt, in his book *A Cup of Trembling*, defies anyone to come up with a plausible reason why Jerusalem — of all the cities in the world — should so occupy the attention of the world's nations. His conclusion, of course, is that it only makes sense in light of biblical prophecies.

Remember also that these verses are not isolated cases. Notice what God has to say in Isaiah 49:26:

> And I will feed them that oppress thee with their own flesh; and they shall be drunken with their own blood, as with sweet wine: and all flesh shall know that I the Lord am thy Saviour and thy Redeemer, the mighty One of Jacob.

If you choose to believe that this is a coincidence, consider Jeremiah 30: 14–16:

> All thy lovers have forgotten thee, they seek thee not. . . . Therefore all they that devour thee shall be devoured; and all thine adversaries, every one of them, shall go into captivity; and they that spoil thee shall be a spoil, and all that prey upon thee will I give for a prey.

Then consider that Middle East analysts are predicting that the United States, heretofore Israel's staunch ally, might be compelled to stand aside in the event of a new Arab-Israeli war for a variety of reasons (oil dependency, weariness of policing foreign conflicts).

Certainly the Babylonians, Assyrians, Romans, Arabs, Crusaders, and Turks have tried to impose their will on this land and to conquer Jerusalem. But never have the *nations of the world* converged as they are at this moment in history.

The long-dead Jewish prophets are trying to get our attention. So is the Psalmist:

> Keep not thou silence, O God: hold not thy peace, and be not still, O God. For lo, thine enemies make a tumult: and they that hate thee have lifted up the head. They have taken crafty counsel against thy people, and consulted against thy hidden ones. They have said, Come, and let us cut them off from being a nation; that the name of Israel may be no more in remembrance. For they have consulted together with one consent: they are confederate against thee (Ps. 83:1–5).

The context of this passage, as well as the others cited, is of a last days scenario, not a past invasion by a pagan power. The very language of Psalm 83 alone so parallels the thoughts, attitudes, and plans of Israel's Middle East neighbors that one can scarcely understand why it isn't a major topic of conversation.

But it isn't a major topic of conversation.

In a museum in Jerusalem's Old City, one can see a plaque on a stone wall, next to a slender window. The plaque quotes Zechariah 2:4:

> Jerusalem shall be inhabited as towns without walls for the multitude of men and cattle therein.

Only in the last hundred or so years has there been any building outside the Old City walls. A Jewish benefactor named Moses Montefeori provided the funds in the mid-19th century for the construction of homes.

As one's eyes move from the plaque to the window, one can see giant cranes operating throughout the modern city of Jerusalem, outside the stone walls, building and building some more, so that the city's burgeoning population will have room to live and grow.

Bible prophecy has very little do with identifying the Antichrist, or other fodder for late-night horror movies. It has everything to do with looking at the Bible with unpopular glasses, reading the warnings as if they are real and approaching.

In a 1999 article, *USA Today* writer Jack Kelley said that most people express surprise that there is a real place called Armageddon, and that it is located in the heart of modern Israel. Most people today assume the legendary battleground is merely the plot for an Arnold Schwarzzeneger movie.

It's a shame that society views the Bible as a collection of myths, legends, and contradictions/mistakes, for something is in the air. The prophets are suddenly highly relevant, their writings fitting not their own times but ours.

The Jews have come back to their land. The nations of the world are agitated with Israel. The Arabs talk of wiping the nation off the face of the earth. As an Egyptian writer put it once:

> God has gathered the Zionists together from the corners of the world so that the Arabs can kill them at one strike. This was impossible before, owing to their dispersion. (Egyptian daily *Al-Ahram*, September 6, 1956).

This quote, so similar to the scenario in Psalm 83, also flies in the face of another Bible verse:

Then the heathen that are left round about you shall know that I the Lord build the ruined places, and plant that that was desolate: I the Lord have spoken it, and I will do it (Ezek. 36:36).

So, someone is going to be wrong. Either the Arabs who wish to rid the world of the Jews, or the God who said he would preserve them forever. That is why the real importance in this issue is not whether the unpredictable oil markets will rob us of our prosperity, but whether we will recognize the Bible for what it really is.

That is why former TV newsman David Brinkley doesn't have it quite right as an ad spokesman for Archer-Daniels-Midland when he says that peace won't come to the earth until we all have enough to eat.

Certainly the Bible tells us to feed the hungry, among other things, but it clearly says that peace will not come to the earth until the Creator returns to establish that elusive peace. TV news anchors, politicans, diplomats, religious leaders, and many millions of "average" people can't see this. And so, we continue to pursue flawed peace strategies. We look in every corner, behind every shelf, but never turn around to look at the middle of the room, where the Bible in all its simplicity stands bearing the truth.

In February 1999, Jordan's King Hussein succumbed to cancer. Eulogizing the leader of desert royalty, U.S. President Bill Clinton said that he was sure that when peace finally comes to the Middle East, the diminutive king will see his name on it. Here the president was abandoning his own religious roots, which embrace the idea that only Messiah will deliver peace.

The president left office to join a vast company of past leaders — all of whom were sure they would cement a historic peace deal between Israel and her Arab neighbors. For none of them have ever been able to see the real solution, the one some of us still wait for.

We then come to this last war, this war with ourselves and how we will see history and reality. Will we awaken in time to see the reality of what Isaiah recorded?

May God let it be so.

NOTES

1   Calvin B. Johnson, *Beyond the Point of No Return* (Danville, VA: Calvin B. Johnson, 1997).

2   Claude Duvernoy, *Controversy of Zion* (Green Forest, AR: New Leaf Press, 1987).

3   John Shelby Spong, *Here I Stand* (New York: Harper San Francisco, 1999).

ARIEL SHARON

Former divisional tank commander; Minister of
Defense; Foreign Minister, Prime Minister

On a balmy March evening in Tel Aviv, I arrived with a
few companions at the office of General Ariel Sharon, the
legendary Israeli soldier and politician.

We passed through metal detectors and were then
seated in a lobby where we waited. Danny Yatom, then
head of the Mossad, Israel's secret service, nodded as he
strode down a hallway
and stopped at the el-
evator.

Finally we were
ushered into Sharon's
office, where we again
waited. Later we discov-
ered that Sharon, a
member of Benjamin
Netanyahu's cabinet,
had been holding secret
talks with the Palestin-
ians.

When Sharon en-
tered through a side
door, he extended a
beefy hand in greeting

Ariel Sharon

and the interview commenced. Dressed in a leather jacket, he forcefully but politely explained the peace process from his point of view. To further illustrate his point, at the conclusion of our discussion he presented us with a map of the West Bank, neatly marked in the blue, green, and red lines of border demarcations.

Sharon, despised by the left and revered by the right, is a hard man by any measure. His stunning tank maneuver in the Sinai Desert at the height of the 1973 Yom Kippur War, very likely kept Israel from being overrun. His handling of the 1982 Lebanon War has been much debated; Sharon was forced to resign as defense minister after heinous murders in two Beirut suburbs were carried out by the Phalange, a Lebanese militia group fighting PLO forces in the city. Many felt that Sharon should have anticipated the revenge killings. Sharon proved in a highly publicized slander suit against *Time* magazine that he had no involvement with the civilian massacres.

Having been born and raised in British-controlled Palestine, Sharon learned early on the dangers of frontier life. Plagued by nightly terrorist raids and attacks on Jewish settlements on the coastal plain, Jews like Sharon patrolled at night to repel attackers.

After the establishment of the state of Israel in 1948, Sharon became a fixture in the Israel Defense Forces, and a particular favorite of Prime Minister David Ben Gurion. Sharon's involvement with the famed Unit 101 commando unit propelled him into the upper echelons of the Israeli military. His service in the 1967 Six Day War prepared him for the fame that came his way some six years later.

Sharon continues to be a lightning rod of controversy. His September 2000 visit to the Temple Mount in Jerusalem assured the 72-year-old Sharon of further headlines.

On Tuesday, February 6, 2001, Ariel Sharon became the 11th prime minister of the state of Israel, defeating Ehud Barak by some 25 percentage points. Only months before, Sharon, long criticized for a litany of alleged abuses of power, was considered politically dead.

When Barak's grip on power was weakened by the Palestinian violence, new elections were called. Many speculated that former Premier Benjamin Netanyahu would enter the fray and reclaim the prime minister's office. However, since Netanyahu had resigned his seat in the Israeli parliament, the Knesset, he was ineligible to run in the special election, which would be for prime minister only.

This twisting development left Sharon, as chairman of the Likud Party, with the inside track to run opposite Barak.

With fighting all over the country escalating, Israelis abandoned Barak's land-for-peace initiatives and embraced the old war-horse Sharon.

The following interview reflects Sharon's long-standing positions on peace for Israel and the Arabs.

David Lewis: It's good to see you again, General Sharon. We are in Israel to gather information for a new book I am writing. It will deal, in part, with Israel's relationship to the media. We are disturbed at the treatment that Israel is getting from the Western media. I would like to thank you for allowing me to interview you once again.

What do you think would be the ideal outcome of the peace process?

Ariel Sharon: First of all, peace — I accept. All of us would like to live in peace. On a very personal level, I have participated in all of the wars and major battles of this country in the last 50 years. I saw the horrors in the fields of war. I saw my friends being killed in these battles. I've had to make decisions of life and death for others and myself. I therefore believe that I understand the importance of peace, maybe better than many of the politicians that speak about peace, but they never had the chance to see the battlefield or to have this awful experience. But for me, peace must also provide security.

David Lewis: Right, absolutely. Peace on paper without security is hollow. It is no peace at all. [This especially comes home to us in the light of the October war of the year 2000. The October war actually began in the midst of U.S.-brokered negotiations which brought Yasser Arafat and Prime Minister Barak together for a series of peace talks.]

Ariel Sharon: If peace doesn't provide security, there is no reason for this peace. Peace should allow one to live a normal life and dedicate our talents for more productive things than fighting. It's a basic thing, however, that we should be ready to defend our families, our homeland. If this had taken place in the beginning, say, for example, from 1948 when the state was founded, if we could have enjoyed 50 years of peace until now, I believe it could have been a different country and a different kind of region.

David Lewis: General, I believe that is absolutely correct. In the Genesis covenant that God made with Abram, the Lord said that Israel would be a blessing to the nations. Can you share with us some ways that peace could bring benefit, not only to Israel, but also for her neighbors as well?

Ariel Sharon: Well, for example, think about how tourism would flourish even better. It would enable us to dedicate ourselves to the better things in life, the more humanitarian side of life. If peace can be accomplished it will be to the benefit not only for Israel, but for the entire region.

I never saw that Israel should feel that we must be the teacher of the whole area. There should be reciprocity, each side learning from the other. We are willing and ready to share our know-how. We are ready to help and would like to be helped.

David Lewis: Do you think the Palestinians will ever be satisfied? Israel has already given away the Sinai, including Taba, Yamit, the strategic Mitla and Jeddi Passes, and the Abu Rudis oil fields. Israel has given away half of the Golan

Heights, Jericho, Bethlehem, and the Gaza Strip, including the city of Gaza.

Now they want Jerusalem. They want all the rest of the Golan, right to the shores of the Sea of Galilee and the West Bank (Judea and Samaria). What if they get this? What then? Will it bring an end to war and terrorism?

Ariel Sharon: I hope, but no, I don't believe they will be satisfied. Well, they'll be satisfied for a while, but take Palestinian demands today. At the present time 30 or 40 percent [of the land] would satisfy them.

But the Muslim fundamentalists, like the Hamas, the Hizbollah, and others, do everything they can to upset the peace process. Now, that's a dangerous situation. They do not want peace. They only want to defeat us and possess all the land.

David Lewis: Is there any hope?

Ariel Sharon: Maybe, when we consider the fact that the younger Palestinian population is larger than the older population. In a sense this might give us cause to hope. Some of the younger Arabs, university students, some of them are becoming softer toward Israel, you know, and they become more interested in Israeli political life. The problem is that they are divided, even those that are interested in making peace with us. I don't think that they are willing to make the adjustments for achieving real peace, like the Arab world in general. They are not ready for reconciliation. It may take 50 years, yet, to make peace. However, it is important that we are talking now. Contact has been established.

David Lewis: Do you think that the Western politicians and media understand the Muslim mentality of jihad [holy war]?

Ariel Sharon: No, I don't think so. As an example, consider the Hamas people like Sheik Yassin, whom Israel released from prison. Yassin said that the Arabs have time on their side. He said that Israel will not exist after the year 2027. Israel has no more than 30 years to exist, because of pressures from the outside, social conflicts, the shallowness of part of the population of Israel within the nation, all that together spells the doom of Israel in 30 to 50 years.

Yasser Arafat and the Palestinian National Authority, on the other hand, don't have much time. They need results now, so they would like to get into an arrangement with Israel, but they are going to try and get all that they want. Israel is willing to compromise, but not to stop breathing. In other words, Israel must not cease to exist.

Israel must look to the future very carefully. We must be very careful not to take unnecessary risks. We must not be so eager to reach an agreement, to make such concessions that would make it much easier for the Arab radicals, who hate us (even the moderates hate us, of course). The United States should not put pressure on Israel, because you live thousands of miles away from this arena of conflict and it is difficult for you to grasp our situation. It is hard for you to imagine the terrorism that hangs over us constantly and the twisted reporting of the media certainly doesn't help the situation.

When the United States of America continues to pressure us for more and more concessions, it encourages the Arab leaders to demand more and more. Some of these concessions would be very dangerous, not only for us, but for our neighbors as well. Yes, we want peace, but it must be peace with security.

I mentioned earlier that some of the Arabs are more moderate toward us for the practical reason that they know that peace would bring prosperity to the whole region. But they are faced by the dilemma that so many Arabs are very hard and they don't want to make any concessions at all. Anyway, we hope for the best and we work toward the day when peace will prevail.

David Lewis: In other words, General Sharon, your con-

THE LAST WAR

cern is for who will win the struggle in the Arab ranks, those like the young people on the campuses of the universities who are in a hurry and are willing to bargain with Israel. Then there are the radical youth who have little interest in talking peace with Israel. Then there is a third group, the old guard, like the Hamas, the Hizbollah, and the Muslim brotherhood. Our question is who shall prevail?

Ariel Sharon: The solution, whatever it is, should be such that would provide Israel time. I thought in the past that we needed an immediate solution, but now I've reconsidered. I think perhaps it is necessary to lower our expectations. I believe that we should try for a temporary state of non-belligerency, where they will have part of the area. We will have to provide them with the possibility to run their lives with less interference from us, as much as possible.

Israel will keep and hold the security areas, especially along the green line (pre-1967 borders). It could be 20 kilometers wide on the east side of the green line and about 10 kilometers on the west side of the green line.

David Lewis: Where do you envision the peace process going now?

Ariel Sharon: I believe peace should go along two tracks. First of all, the political track, that involves negotiation about borders and fences and so on. On the other track is the humanitarian side, where we build relationships, cooperation with security, the economy, welfare, education, and so on. Then we'll see what it is going to bring us.

David Lewis: Surely this would not mean a return to the pre-1967 borders?

Ariel Sharon: I can see you understand our problems. Yes, Dr. Lewis, we always strive for peace, all the time recognizing the dangers involved. It would be very dangerous at this time to even talk about a return to the pre-1967 borders.

David Lewis: General Sharon, in the West the media always talks about the occupied territories. . . .

Ariel Sharon: Yes, occupied territories, but who are the occupiers? Israel did not occupy the territories from 1948 to 1967, so who were the occupiers? The answer is Jordan and Syria. Israel was willing to settle for a lot less land than she ended up with after the 1948 war of independence. Jordan seized all of the land that should have provided the Palestinians with a nation of their own. Israel received a mandate over the land when we took it legitimately in the 1967 war. Even now it is not exactly accurate to speak of the population as being "occupied." Indeed, 98 percent of the Palestinian population is under Palestinian control. Only 2 percent is under Israeli control. That's the situation.

David Lewis: The Western media continually lies about Israel. What we read in the press in America and Canada is such distortion and violation of truth. In a sense we are getting used to that in the West. We say, "Well, that's the media." What is shocking for us is to come here as American Christian Zionists and find that the local Israeli media is full of the same kind of distortion. What can be said about this?

Ariel Sharon: Nothing good can be said about this, but you've seen it for yourself.

Look, what can I say about the press? First of all, the press is connected. They tend to listen to each other and say the same thing.

David Lewis: But it seems as if the Israeli press is so self-destructive. They are almost anti-Zionist aren't they?

Ariel Sharon: It is a real problem here, and I don't want to overstate the case, but it is true that even in the Israeli press we have a major problem, a major problem.

David Lewis: Well, we hope with this book to allow Israel to tell her own story. I wrote a book about the Lebanon

War in 1982 which went all over the world. It was translated into German and other languages. We're hoping that this current book will offset some of the lies and some of the distortions of the media. We don't want to be seen as attacking Israel, and yet we can't be silent about the extremist left-wing socialist press and their anti-Zionist attitudes. So we have to address this in the book, and yet we don't want to come off looking as if we are against Israel. It is a very big problem to all of us, I guess.

Ariel Sharon: It is a very difficult problem for us as well. Now, Israel is more of a democracy than a democracy [Israel's unique government policies include allowing almost limitless press freedoms; and Arab-Israelis loyal to the PNA serving in the Knesset], you know, and we have a problem here. You see what's already happened here. Part of the Jews became weaker, yet the state of Israel is much stronger now than in the past.

David Lewis: Yes.

Ariel Sharon: But the fact is that part of the Jews in Israel became weaker, and they became weaker due to the fact that their roots became too shallow.

David Lewis: Because they abandoned Judaism.

Ariel Sharon: They went away from Judaism.

David Lewis: That's right.

Ariel Sharon: Many of them don't know the Bible. They don't know anything about Jewish wisdom. They don't know the history of Israel or of the Jewish people. They don't have the feeling of how to express full rights to the land — it's just not in their souls. And that's how we became weaker, that's what happened. But on the other hand, many of the strong Orthodox people who are believers in Zion are getting more and more involved. For example, in the army you see many men and boys wearing a kippah, and they are moving up the ranks into the elite positions. They are becoming stronger, whereas some of the secular Jews became weaker in their Zionism and patriotism.

David Lewis: It is just like what Charles Dickens wrote in his classic novel *A Tale of Two Cities:* "It was the best of times, it was the worst of times."

Ariel Sharon: You know, Zionism was a giant revolution. It has brought Jews from all over the earth. There were already thousands of Jews living here in the land, but Zionism brought millions to these borders, and molded them into one nation. I believe that we can look at the future with optimism.

David Lewis: That's good.

Ariel Sharon: Israel's first priority is to bring Jews home to this country. We believe that there is still, potentially, a million newcomers who will come from the former Soviet Union, and they are coming.

David Lewis: Yes, they are. You know, General Sharon, this is exactly what was prophesied by Jeremiah, "Therefore, behold, the days come, saith the LORD, that it shall no more be said, The LORD liveth, that brought up the children of Israel out of the land of Egypt; But, The LORD liveth, that brought up the children of Israel *from the land of the north*, and from all the lands whither he had driven them: and I will bring them again into their land that I gave unto their fathers" (Jer. 16:14–15, italics added).

Ariel Sharon: Yes, and there are hundreds of thousands of Jews in France, and millions in America. Our main effort should be to persuade them to make *aliyah*. [Aliyah is a Hebrew word that means "to return to the land."] We need to allocate not only the means but also the will and desire and determination to provide education. We need to teach the Bible and the Hebrew language, the story of the Jewish heroes. This is what preserves our Jewish heritage, and that will keep them coming back to the land of Israel.

David Lewis: You know this media problem isn't new. I think back to 1982. I took a group of journalists into Lebanon with IDF forces as protection, and I came out and wrote a book about the Lebanon War, in defense of Israel's actions there. It was outrageous what they said about Shatilla and Sabra. The way you were smeared and slandered in the general media and especially *Time* magazine was absolutely untenable. I recall the first time I ever met you and interviewed you in 1982. You were being heavily attacked by the American media for allegedly leading the "massacre" at Shatilla and Sabra in Lebanon in which 460 Palestinians, including 35 women and children were killed.[1] You were being unjustly blamed for this tragedy.[2]

Ariel Sharon: Well, actually no Israelis were involved in the event. It was Christian Arabs killing Muslim Arabs, but I was blamed for it. I think I must be the first minister of defense in history who had to leave the battlefield and go back to work on his farm because of Arabs killing their own brothers and cousins.

Avigdor Rosenberg: It was retaliation between the Muslims and the Christians. That's why the Christians killed the Muslims.

David Lewis: The Muslims had murdered most of the people living in the Maronite Christian town of Damour,[3] Lebanon. It was the Damour Brigade that went in and did the killing at Shatilla and Sabra, near Beirut. Their motive was revenge.

Ariel Sharon: Let me tell you about the massacre in Lebanon. There was a question as to whether it should be called a massacre. Of course, every life lost was a tragedy. It was an attack against those forces that were trying to overthrow the democratically elected government of Lebanon.

At this point (around 8:15 p.m.) General Sharon was handed a note by Mr. Ra'anan Gissan, his assistant. He was noticeably excited by what he read, and after apologies for cutting our interview short, he excused himself.

The next day after the interview we read in the paper that the night before, Sharon was called away from a meeting to meet Crown Prince Abdullah of Jordan (now the King of Jordan).

NOTES

1   This is the figure finally given by the Red Cross, which is certainly not known for any pro-Israel bias. Quite to the contrary, most knowledgable Middle Eastern researchers recognize the anti-Zionist attitudes of the Red Cross organization.

2   Aharoni, Dov, *General Sharon's War Against Time Magazine: His Trial and Vindication* (New York: Shapolsky/Steimatzky, 1985), p. 90. The extraordinary story of the legendary hero who took on the TIME empire — and won! He fought a lengthy battle for his vindication in one of the landmark trials of American history — and in the process gained the respect and admiration of millions of Americans.

3   David Allen Lewis, *Magog 1982 Canceled* (Green Forest, AR: New Leaf Press, 1982), p. 54–61.

DAVID BAR-ILLAN

Journalist, political commentator

Bar-Illan, director of public policy and planning for the Netanyahu government from 1996–99, is a long-time friend. For many years a concert pianist, Bar-Illan has also enjoyed a distinguished journalism career, serving as editor of the *Jerusalem Post*, where his popular and controversial "Eye on the Media" column generated a wide readership.

We conducted this interview at Bar-Illan's Jerusalem office, in the Prime Minister's Bureau. The heavy security necessary to secure a spot in David's office was a sober reminder of the violent times in which we live. A considerable wait, even after a phone call from David's office, brought to reality the complexities of the Middle East.

David Bar-Illan

After Yitzhak Rabin's horrific murder in November 1995, some security details came under considerable criticism; hence, the enormous security measures the average citizen must undertake even to chat with an old friend.

David Lewis: I've been commissioned by my publisher, New Leaf Press, to do a book, allowing Israel to tell her own story through her leadership, in answer to certain charges done by the Western media against Israel — misrepresentations, distortions, and so forth in the press. I'd primarily like for this to be your book by you and all the leadership of Israel. We want to be your spokespeople; we're going to be your mouthpiece to the world. We're not slanting this one. This is the first book I've ever done that's not slanted exclusively to a religious audience. It's going to be a book that will appeal to both secular and religious audiences. We want to get your statements and opinions on a variety of subjects and then we'll go back to the facts you've been giving to flesh it out — as far as Har Homa is concerned, the temple tunnel turmoil, and so on.

Some subjects we have already listed that we want to cover are the Oslo accords, of course, and the PLO Covenant, the Palestinian National Authority's non-compliance, and the media. We would also like to discuss the Temple Mount incident, the riot on the tunnel, the settlements, Har Homa, and Israel's non-retaliation in the Gulf War, which we feel has never been accredited properly in the press to Israel's credit.

David Bar-Illan: Right . . . right.

David Lewis: We might also get into Holocaust revisionism, and a denial of persecution of Christians in the West Bank.

David Bar-Illan: Okay. Well, we haven't touched on the Palestinians. You see the main problem here is not so much what we have or have not done, but the fact that you have Palestinians who are obviously great sympathizers and supporters of Saddam Hussein. They call for the destruction of Israel and also refuse to change their convenant. Their refusal to change the covenant, in context, is much worse than just a plain refusal. When you have demonstrations calling for the destruction of Israel at the same time, you get a different [point of view], you get it in context. Another factor that would give it a better perspective is a celebration, commemoration I should say, by the Palestinians of what they call "the Great Disaster," meaning the establishment of the state of Israel. They are commemorating it, parallel to our celebrations of the 50th anniversary of the state of Israel. They are commemorating "the great disaster" of the establishment of the state of Israel.

David Lewis: I've heard about this, but I really don't know much about it.

David Bar-Illan: Well, Arafat is organizing it. It's not something that's done by some rogue operation. This is Arafat himself, with all the authority of the Palestinian National Authority, and with the organization calling for celebrations to be held by Palestinians throughout the year everywhere. Now this includes the Arabs of Israel, and that is really quite an incongruous business because the Arabs of Israel are actually commemorating "the great disaster" of the establishment of the state of which they are citizens.

It also shows a certain inability to admit mistakes, because the great disaster of 50 years ago (and it was a great disaster for the Palestinians), was a direct result of their refusal to accept a compromise, of their decision to try to destroy Israel in its embryonic state before it actually became a state. If only they had admitted what happened, that Israel, in reality, existed as a nation, think of the benefits that would have proceeded from this admission. They could have become a state. They could have lived in prosperity. They could have avoided the killings of thousands of people on both sides, the displacement of hundreds of thousands of Palestinians, being condemned to live in camps for the next 50 years. All that could have been avoided simply by accepting a compromise. Instead of now saying, "We were wrong. We didn't accept a compromise. We chose the way of violence. We chose the way of terrorism and war instead of the compromise of peace that could have led to genuine lasting peace."

They're saying "the Great Disaster" was the establishment of the state of Israel. That could have brought to them unprecedented prosperity, and for the first time in their history, they would have had independence. For the first time in their history they would have had self-determination, self-definition, and the first time in their history in which they would have been really prosperous, almost overnight. And so, that is what worries me more than anything else. This total inability to learn from history really reminds you of what Santiana said — that those who refuse to learn from history are condemned to relive it. It's just a terrible phenomenon. And when it's combined with the call on Saddam Hussein to destroy Tel Aviv and with the refusal to change a covenant which is a genocidal covenant — the only one that I know of in existence in the world today, a charter...a national charter which calls for the destruction of another people, instead of calling for some kind of construction on the part of the people who have written the charter. When you take all that in combination you realize that something is very wrong here and to call them a fitting partner for peace may be an overstatement.

David Lewis: We're dealing with a lot of historical revisions in this whole situation, aren't we? A refusal to recognize the past.

David Bar-Illan: Well, what you're touching on is an even larger problem. And that is, in order to justify the call for the destruction of Israel, you have to change history, because history . . . justifies the state of Israel perhaps more than it justifies any existence of any state in the world. Not only does history justify the unprecedented unique connection between the Jewish people and the land of Israel, not only does it make a right of the Jews to this country irrefutable, it makes the Palestinian claim for this state totally irrelevant. So you have to change history. And the effort to change history has been revoltingly successful.

We are not only witnessing here the denial of the Holocaust, which is something that at least for now is still unacceptable in most polite circles, we are witnessing a total . . . fictionalization . . . not only a distortion, a fictionalization of the facts. The Palestinians are now claiming not only that Jesus was a Palestinian rather than a Jew (a Judean born in Judea, you know), they are now claiming that they are descendants of the Canaanites and the Philistines, and the Jebusites. The Jebusites were actually a sort of branch of the Canaanites. They're claiming that they are the descendants of those people, which means that they were here before the Jews, and that they were actually displaced from their land by the Jews — something that, on the face of it, is so ridiculous that you feel almost demeaned trying to attack it because it is so childish. But, amazingly enough, a respectable publication like the *National Geographic* actually repeats this claim in a serious vein. Not as a ridiculous notion, not as a ridiculous supposition or claim by someone, but as something to be taken seriously.

I am not in any way inclined to underestimate the power of such big lies. Because we've learned in this century that the very fact of the very fast information that we have, instead of actually illuminating the truth, makes possible the dissemination of lies. We've seen this throughout this century and the more information becomes instantaneous and at your fingertips, the more distorted it can become. This is the amazing thing about it. Now, the Palestinians obviously have a problem because if they are the descendants of those people, they can't also be Arabs. I mean, the Arabs invaded this country in the 7th century, so how can you be Arabs at the same time that you are Canaanites or Philistines or Jebusites or whatever it is. But they manage to do it. They manage somehow to combine the two and tell these "Arabian Nights" stories to serious people, serious correspondents, serious journalist people who are at least educated enough to know better and to have them repeated with all seriousness. And this is what is so worrisome and that touches on what you've said. Because what you're saying is that history has to be rewritten in order to justify the, delegitimation of Israel, but there you are.

David Lewis: Let's go back to the 1800s. What was it like here?

David Bar-Illan: Well, I think that the best thing to do is to read people like Mark Twain who were in this country in the 19th century. The point is that he was obviously a very objective observer in this country and what he described was a country in ashes, totally barren, swamp-ridden.

David Lewis: He said that it was a blighted and a blasted land.

David Bar-Illan: That's exactly right, and of course, only he could describe this well. But his descriptions are precisely what every missionary and tourist and writer and pilgrimage maker in this country wrote at the time. And there were quite a few. The Holy Land has always attracted people, and quite a few described exactly what was going on in this country, or rather to be more accurate, what was not going on this country. It was really a desert and a swamp and nothing more. And that is precisely the way the first pioneers, the first Zionists who came here with my great-grandfather 110 years ago, described it too. This is exactly what they found here, and they died like flies from malaria because the place was nothing but swamps full of swarms of these mosquitoes which spread the disease. My grandfather's descriptions of this country match exactly what Mark Twain wrote.

David Lewis: Do you have any family letters or documents left over from that period of time?

David Bar-Illan: My father was an engineer, an electric engineer, and he built the first high-tension wire in this country. The stories that he told and wrote in his diary are just extraordinary. I remember from my childhood going to areas of this country, vast areas of this country which are now very thickly populated, which were absolutely nothing.

There was absolutely nothing there. I remember writing a composition for my fifth grade, maybe, about a tour around the country. Even in my time (we're talking about the thirties) there was very little here. The real boom began then, in the thirties, and has continued, fortunately, since then with the constant growth.

It was then also that the vast Arab immigration began because of the availability of jobs, the availability of opportunities in this country, which was so vastly superior to anything in neighboring countries. There was no limitation on their immigration, while there was a tremendous amount of limitation, a very strict limitation on Jewish immigration, by the British authority.

David Lewis: The first aliyah [the return to the land, literally *the ascent*] of major proportions took place in the 1800s. What year did that start?

David Bar-Illan: In the 1880s the Bilu Aliyah took place. This movement was parallel to the time that my great-grandfather came here, but he was not part of that movement. The first aliyah was in the end of the 19th century; the second aliyah was before the First World War.

David Lewis: Did the Arab population begin to increase at that time?

David Bar-Illan: The Arab population was static up to that point. The increase of Arab population was caused by the kind of environment produced here by the Zionists. They saw the new prosperity of the land, the working environment mostly, the job environment. And also the living environment was a completely different kind of story from what it had been before. It was a forlorn, abandoned, neglected desert and swamp, as I said before, but it began to become a civilized area as soon as the pioneers, the Jews, came here.

We still attract hundreds of thousands of Arabs here to this country. Not all of them can come, not all of them can enter, but tens of thousands certainly do. We have Egyptians here, we have Jordanians here, we have Saudis here. We have everybody coming into the country as tourists, and under all sorts of guises — sometimes illegally. Sometimes they simply infiltrate, they remain here, they work here. Jordanian tourists come into this country never to be seen again, at least not in Jordan. They simply remain here to work. And that's inevitable.

David Lewis: How many foreign workers?

David Bar-Illan: A quarter of a million foreign workers, of whom 100,000 are legal and the other 150,000 just infiltrated into the country. And I'm not talking about Palestinians or Arabs. We're talking about the people from Thailand, Nigeria, Portugal, and Romania.

David Lewis: Exactly what, in your view, did the Balfour Declaration of 1917 actually promise to the Jewish people?

David Bar-Illan: Look — after the Turkish Empire was carved out, the British decided to create a Pax Britannia in this area, a place that would be controlled by the British and to some extent by the French, but mostly by the British. They divided it between themselves and the French. Because of many debts that they owed the Jewish people during the First World War in general, they decided to give the area that is now known as Israel and the West Bank and Jordan — all that area — for a Jewish national home. One of the debts was to Chaim Wietzman, who was the head of the Zionist movement at the time and a chemist who invented a form of synthetic coal, which was attributed to have saved Britain during the winters of the First World War.

David Lewis: So the whole thing — the West Bank, the East Bank, everything — was supposed to be a Jewish national homeland.

David Bar-Illan: East Bank, West Bank, everything. The size of Jordan, as you know, is four-fifths of the whole thing. So the area of the kingdom of Jordan is four times larger than the West Bank and Israel, from the Jordan River to the sea. But let me mention something else here. The British did that, and you would say, "Well, the British Empire was the only great power at the time after the war. They defeated Germany and they defeated Turkey, and the Ottoman Empire was being divided by the victors." But that wasn't the whole story, you see. The only reason the British got international approval, international sanction for the dominance in this part of the world, for the hegemony in this part of the world, was because they gave this area to be the Jewish national home. Because of the Balfour Declaration, the League of Nations gave the mandate to the British.

David Lewis: Let's talk about the Peel Commission. What was their action and what year was that? Was that 1936?

David Bar-Illan: 1936, yeah. I remember that very well, actually. The interesting thing about the Peel Commission is not that the British again tried to cut the country, to partition the country into an Arab state and a Jewish state. That wasn't to me the most outstanding feature of those hearings, which as you know didn't amount to anything. To me, the interesting part, particularly in light of what we said at the beginning of this conversation, was that the Palestinians, or those who now call themselves Palestinians, adamantly denied that they were Palestinians. They appeared before the Peel Commission. The leading Arab historian of that time, Philip Hittie, said that Palestinians are Jews, *we are not Palestinians, we are Arabs, we are part of the great Arab nation.* We [Jews] called ourselves Palestinians, you know. As you probably remember, before I became an editor of the *Jerusalem Post*, I made a career as a pianist for 50 years. My first publicity brochures had me as a Palestinian pianist because there was no state of Israel yet. I was working for a newspaper that is called [today] the *Jerusalem Post*, but until 1950, which means two years after the establishment of Israel, it was called the *Palestine Post*. The orchestra with which I played as soloist was called the Palestine Symphony. It is now known as the Israeli Philharmonic Orchestra, but at that time it was known as the Palestine Symphony.

David Lewis: So the Jews were the Palestinians?

David Bar-Illan: ONLY the Jews were the Palestinians. The others were Arabs. They always called themselves Arabs. Not a single institution, even the most nationalistic Arab institution in this country, was called Palestinian. It was always called Arab — the Arab High Council, the Arab High Command, the Arab this, and the Arab that. Palestinian was a taboo word for the Arabs of this country. It was used only by the Jews. The Zionist Jews in America used to sing "Palestine, Palestine, oh my Palestine."

David Lewis: When did all this change? When did they [Arabs] become Palestinians?

David Bar-Illan: It's very difficult to pinpoint, but I would say towards the end of the 1950s and the beginning of the 1960s.

David Lewis: Well, let's come up to the present. Two incidents always loom large when the media wants to historically damn Israel — that's the massacre at Deir Yassin and the bombing of the King David [Hotel]. Can you comment on those two incidents?

David Bar-Illan: Yes . . . even some Arab scholars, Palestinian scholars, now admit that all the numbers about Deir Yassin were at least double what they actually were. And I think that any kind of an assessment of what happened would reach the inevitable conclusion that there was absolutely no massacre whatsoever. Furthermore, the attacking force warned everybody to evacuate, to clear out. As a result of this warning they lost the element of surprise and four of the attackers were killed. Again, when four of the attackers are killed, it's hardly a massacre. It's obviously a battle. Many were injured. But the main problem in Deir Yassin is one which repeated itself over and over again during what is known as the Riots of 1936–39 and later in the War of Lebanon in the early eighties — the habit of hiding behind children and women was ubiquitous; not only prevalent, but ubiquitous. In Lebanon, as you know, they would have children seated on windowsills with the soldiers, or the fighters of the PLO, shooting from behind them, knowing full well that the Israeli soldiers would have trouble shooting at children sitting on windowsills. Instead of having sandbags there, they would have children. Same thing happened in Deir Yassin. When the warning to evacuate came about, they simply didn't let about 100 women and children go away.

That it is what caused the casualties among the women and children. The British described it all the time as fighting against Arab villages. As bad as the British sometimes were as a colonial power, they felt it was the most horrendous brutality to hide behind women and children when shooting and forcing them [the British] to shoot civilians in order to get to the terrorists on the other side. So, this is really the story. The fact is that there was no massacre. Witnesses with the perspective of time deny these stories, even though at that time they succumbed to the implorations of Arab propagandists and told all sorts of stories of how they were murdered. The fact is that despite this, despite the non-massacre nature of what happened there, the Arabs of Palestine believe that it did happen and in a way it boomeranged as nothing else during that war boomeranged. I mean they told stories of naked Arab women paraded through the streets of Jerusalem by the Jews, you know, that sort of thing. Absolutely hair-raising horror stories that were spread all over the place.

David Lewis: With all of the oil wealth the Arabs nations possess, why couldn't they have just assimilated these people [Arab refugees of war] into their own ranks rather than keep them in the camps?

David Bar-Illan: They never wanted to, except for Jordan, which gave citizenship to most of them. But the [other] Arab regimes always resisted. By Arab regimes I mean Syria, Lebanon, the Gulf States, and to a certain extent Lebanon and Egypt. None of them wanted to do anything for them. Nor did the oil rich countries want to contribute towards their welfare, mostly because they felt that they could be used as a political football. They could be used as something that would be used against Israel on the political level. And indeed it was. It's still a threat.

And when you think, by contrast, of the fact that 800,000 Jews had to leave Arab countries because of that war, and that 600,000 of them were absorbed in Israel (200,000 went to European countries) you realize the dimension of the crime against those refugees.

For 50 years, meaning two and a half generations, they had to live in, still have to live in, shanty towns. They're called refugee camps, but they really are, as you've seen yourself, shanty towns, in the worst possible conditions, for no reason whatsoever. They could have very easily been absorbed into the countries which hosted them, and they could have very easily become useful citizens like the Jews from Arab countries who became very useful citizens in Israel.

David Lewis: And what about the bombing of the King David Hotel?

David Bar-Illan: My uncle was in the King David when it was bombed. He was thrown against a wall, very slightly injured. It was not the King David Hotel obviously. It had been the King David Hotel before, and it became the King

David Hotel after. But at that time, it was the headquarters of the British government and police.

David Lewis: So it wasn't being used as a hotel at all?

David Bar-Illan: Not at all. The British administration housed itself in that hotel and mostly it was the headquarters of the police and some army contingents. They were warned 40 minutes before the bomb went off, and Mr. Shaw, I don't remember his first name, was a commander of the British police at the time in Palestine. He said, "I came here to give orders to the Jews, not to take orders from them," and refused to evacuate. As a result, 90 people were killed. Many of them, by the way, were Jews who worked for the British government and for the British police. But it was not a hotel. It was the most legitimate target one can imagine in any kind of war against an occupying army. It was not aimed at civilians and there was ample warning given to save all lives, not just those of innocent bystanders.

David Lewis: On the King David, what do you think was the prime thing that caused the Irgun [a Jewish resistance group] to retaliate in this fashion? What were they angry about with the British; was there something specific that happened?

David Bar-Illan: The war against the British occupying forces here was waged because the British were responsible for the death of anywhere between half a million and a million Jews. There's no question about that. In 1941, when the *Struma*, a ship that left Romania with 700 refugees, was refused entry to British-controlled Palestine and was let go out to sea, it was sunk by a German submarine. As a result, they all drowned. It began then, but it went on. Many such ships were lost at sea — were either torpedoed or sank because they couldn't survive in the high seas [they weren't seaworthy]. And the fact is that many could have survived. Many could have been saved, especially before the end of the war.

David Lewis: There were other incidents with ships, weren't there?

David Bar-Illan: Oh, many, many. There was one that I saw myself. It was called the *Patria*, was brought to Palestine, and refused entry. It actually entered Haifa Harbor and the British refused to let the 1,500 refugees disembark. The refugees were so afraid of being put out to sea again that they bombed the ship, they bombed themselves. The ship sank in Haifa Harbor and over 1,000 people were killed. Such incidents tore the hearts out of the Jewish population here. They wanted either British policy to change or to make it change, or to kick the British out of here. Some believed in doing it diplomatically. Some believed in doing it through force. And diplomacy didn't do very much good, actually, and force seemed to work better. And that was the reason the Irgun began its fighting against the British immediately after the war.

Jim Fletcher: There seems to be a general feeling that there was a shift in the reportage of Israel after the 1967 war. Is that correct?

David Bar-Illan: Yes, of course. None of these things ever happen overnight, but there was a change of mood after the 1967 war. And I think that this is due mainly to two reasons — one is the more immediate reason, and that is, until 1967, when the whole Arab world had declared that it wanted Israel thrown into the sea and when the conflict was portrayed as between Israel and the Arab regimes, the Arab world at that time constituted of something like 150 million people. We were four million at that time here, less than that. We were obviously the David against the Arab Goliath.

When we won that war in a very dramatic, decisive manner, it became difficult to view us as David. And not too slowly, the roles began to change. Particularly because the Arab propaganda machine (and I take my hat off to it for this) managed to change the conflicts from the Arab regimes versus Israel, to Israel versus the Palestinians. And of course in that scenario we became the Goliaths, and the Palestinians the oppressed Davids.

I often describe the mentality, the perception of the conflict since 1967 as the Algeria-Alabama syndrome. For some reason, we are portrayed by many of the Western media as either the colonialists like the French in Algeria, the colonialists who invaded this area and displaced the natives, or as the "haves" against the "have-nots" in a racist kind of situation as in Alabama — we are the whites and the Arabs are the blacks. Either way, nothing could be further from the truth, of course. We didn't displace anyone. And if anything, there's been a ceaseless campaign by the Arab nations against us which calls for our destruction. There has been absolutely no letup in the Arab pronounced-and-declared aim to destroy the state of Israel and to wipe it off the map. That is hardly the picture you get from the press. That is why we so insist on the abolition of the Palestinian Covenant, because that is the expression of that general Arab desire. That is the forefront, the spearhead of that desire to destroy us. It has 33 articles, 30 of which call for our delegitimation and destruction. So, this is the real picture.

The picture that you get from the press is what I described before, as if we are both colonialists and oppressive racists. Now that is the more obvious short-term explanation for the change in media attitude after '67.

There's also another one. After the Second World War, when the revelations of the extent and enormity of the Holocaust became clear to the world, it was very difficult for the world to be anti-Israel. Israel represented the Jews of the world and the national expression of the Jews of the world. And therefore it was difficult to be opposed to it — in the aftermath of the Holocaust, when the whole world, including the Western world, felt a certain amount of guilt

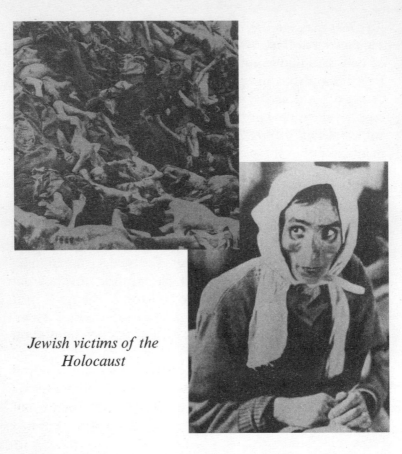

*Jewish victims of the
Holocaust*

and responsibility for the advent of the Holocaust. As time
wore on, a new generation grew up which wasn't aware of
the Holocaust, at least not as acutely as its parents were.
This feeling of responsibility towards what happened to
the Jews faded away and the license to attack Israel became more and more pronounced.

I generally hold that anti-Semitism, which is, as you
know, an age-old disease, has existed for a long time. It
precedes Christianity. It's a phenomenon that many people
have tried to explain and very few have succeeded in ex-
plaining. Nobody can really quite fathom or explain the
whole of it, but it is a phenomenon. It is a phenomenon

which exists in the world today and takes the form of anti-Israelism or anti-Zionism.

It is still unfashionable to be an anti-Semite. Nobody likes to be called an anti-Semite, but it is perfectly permissible to be anti-Israel and anti-Zionist, and so the feelings of anti-Semitism have been channeled into the state of Israel. It's very difficult for people to admit it, but we are held to what some people call a higher standard. This is only another version of the old double standard to which Jews were held. When they say, "Actually, we're flattering you, we're complimenting you, by holding you to higher moral standards than we hold the Arabs," for instance. Or, "When a Jew kills an Arab, its news. When an Arab kills a Jew, it's practically not news at all because we expect it of an Arab, and that is, in a way, a form of flattery. We don't expect this kind of behavior from you and that is why it is news. When you kill or when something like this happens it is man bites dog. When an Arab kills, it's dog bites man. It's not news."

When you examine this kind of flattery or this kind of higher standard carefully, you realize that it is nothing but a double standard because there are many things that Israel does naturally, as all nations do, in order to protect itself, in order to defend itself. The things that are not only forgiven, but are taken for granted in every other nation are immediately ostracized, let alone criticized, when Jews or Israelis do it, or Israel does it as a state.

That's what I think explains the change between the pre-'67 mood of the press, although none of this, of course, is more than a generalization. There are exceptions before '67 and exceptions after the '67 war. There were many anti-Israel people before the war and also much of this sentiment was seen in the press. There are also pro-Israel people like you and others after '67 who keep us bolstered and encouraged. But the proportion is different from what it was, and now today you're perfectly right in saying that a majority of the media seems to be anti-Israel, at least very highly, acutely critical of Israel, while only a minority takes a sympathetic view of what we're doing here.

Jim Fletcher: I'm going to shift away for a minute and then come back to Israel specifically. Unfortunately, in publishing in the USA we have to deal with American narcissism. In Washington last fall you spoke on terrorism. You mentioned something I want to get into. Let's think about the Iranian threat to the United States, because if you can first show Americans how it affects them and then apply the problem to their ally in the Middle East then it starts to sink in. So what are some of the direct threats to the United States from this region in the next few years?

David Bar-Illan: Let me first make one thing clear. Many, especially in the Arab world, try to say to Americans, "The reason you may be exposed to danger, whether it's terrorist danger or direct missile danger" (and this is not so remote nowadays because if Iran acquires the technology to build missiles, it will be able to build intercontinental ballistic missiles within less than a decade which will be able to reach the United States), "is because you are pro-Israeli." The fact is that it is precisely the opposite. All Middle Eastern terrorism is aimed at the West. It is aimed against Western culture, against Western civilization. We, Israel, are attacked because we represent that West to the Arab world and we are here. We are closer. It's easier to attack us, and we are what they call a sword in the side of the body of Islam. We are the bone in their throat. We are here. We are immediate. And we, by their standards, occupy what they consider land of Islam because it was once occupied by Islam. And any land that was once occupied by Islam belongs to Islam, according to their beliefs.

That is why we are the targets — because we are Western, not the other way around. So once you understand that, you realize that no matter what American policy may be (and I have, of course, easy proof of that), it will not placate, it will not pacify, it will not appease those who want to terrorize the West. On the contrary, it will only encourage. For instance, if American policy changes into becoming totally anti-Israeli and pro-Palestinian or pro-Arab, it will not change the fact of terrorist intentions. I can prove this very easily because the European countries thought that was precisely what they would be able to do. The Western nations would become very pro-Arab, pro-Palestinian, anti-Israeli and thereby save themselves from terrorism. But of course, it didn't happen at all. They were subjected to the same kind of terrorism that the Americans were in this part of the world and sometimes in America itself as you know from the World Trade Center bombing. Therefore, what I'm trying to say is that the danger of terrorism to the Western world will continue unless these regimes are somehow curbed and unless they discover it would be more costly to attack Western targets than not to attack them.

That is why we always advocate that the thrust of American policy should be to encourage the democratic elements in this area and to try to contain and sometimes fight those elements which promote violence, war, terrorism — the most recent example is Saddam Hussein, but to which classification the Ayatollahs of Iran also fall. When you ask more specifically about the dangers, of course, you know what terrorist dangers are, from the experience in the United States. I think it was very lucky that the gang that was involved in the World Trade Center bombing was caught in time. Because, as you know, they planned to attack subways, they planned to attack tunnels. Even in the World Trade Center they could have caused thousands of casualties. It was sheer luck that only six people were killed and a thousand injured. It could have been a thousand killed and ten thousand injured. Even the experience of the Japanese terrorists who attacked in the Japanese subway system with a sarin nerve gas also indicates to what extent these terrorists can go. The introduction of easily manufactured non-conventional arms — particularly chemical and biological arms — is also an added danger because it is no longer a question of planting explosives, even though those too can be extremely effective. As you know, a car bomb killed 125 people in one attack in Argentina, in Buenos Aires. This was also done by Middle Eastern terrorists. But what can be done with anthrax and other biological weapons by terrorists is quite mind boggling. And of course, nerve gas and other ingredients can very easily be carried in a suitcase. Carrying a microbes gas canister that can really devastate a place like a subway or a closed hall or gathering area has become a fearsome reality.

Jim Fletcher: A few months ago we were surprised by a column in which the writer compared Mr. Netanyahu and Bill Clinton by saying, among other things, that neither one had any military experience. Do you feel that attitude comes from ignorance or is there an anti-Israel agenda there?

David Bar-Illan: Well, I don't know if the writer has an anti-Israel agenda, but obviously, let's say the writer's erudition, is a bit lacking. Mr. Netanyahu was not only in one of the elite units of the Israeli army and a captain in the army who served in wars here, but also participated in some of the most daring, if not daredevil actual operations in the history of this country.

He was injured in one of them, and by now it's possible at least to tell about two of these. One is the liberating of the passengers of the Sabina plane which was kidnapped by terrorists and landed in the Ben Gurion Airport. He was injured in that operation.

The other was the bombing of the planes in the Beirut Airport and a few other operations in Lebanon which have not yet been revealed, but which everybody knows about. It shows you though, you may be right in suggesting that maybe there is some kind of a bias in it because of these mistakes which seem to be on the face of it. There is never a mistake made that would make Israel look better. It's always a *mistake* that's made, of course; it's an innocent mistake presumably, but it always manages to make Israel look worse or make Netanyahu look worse (as if he didn't serve in the army and therefore he has no military knowledge and doesn't know anything about war). I imagine that we should be lucky that the writer you speak of didn't say anything about his "not inhaling."

Jim Fletcher: Well, my next question is kind of a follow-up to the previous question. Just after Mr. Netanyahu was elected, *Time* magazine ran a story in which they put photographs of possible cabinet members, and under Ariel Sharon's photograph, they called him a "truculent extremist." Then a few months later, after a summit at the White House, they quoted a White House official as saying, "Well, as far as the peace process goes, it's up to Israel how Israel wants to live," implying that it's Israel's fault again. Where does that mentality come from? Do you think it is from the media in general, whether Western or otherwise?

David Bar-Illan: I think that what I said before, about the tendency to look at Israel as a combination of colonialists and racist oppressors, is the syndrome which is perhaps the common denominator for many of the correspondents here. Once they are a captive of this kind of a perception, they adjust the facts to fit it — not the other way around. So, any facts that happen to get in the way of the concept are discarded. The facts which tend to prove it or to support it, or to reinforce it, are the ones that are mentioned or the ones that are brought about, whether they are actual facts or just stories that you hear from people.

By now I think that everybody realizes that nobody is less extreme or less of an extremist than Sharon. He's a very practical man, a very pragmatic man and has always been that way. But that's one of those reputations that is built for people which has very little to do with the truth. In fact, I'm considered one of those people who makes

Genghis Khan look like a hot liberal, but I doubt whether that is correct. And we get used to it. There is a prevalence, particularly in the media of left-wingers. Think of the popularity of Fidel Castro among the media in America and other places, and remember that Mao Zedong and others like him were heroes of the media, not to mention Stalin (of course, I'm the only one old enough around here who remembers that Stalin used to be a great hero of the media). And, as I say, more recently in the memory of the younger generation, people like Castro and Mao Zedong and Che Guevara — for heaven's sakes, he was a big hero. These are thugs and murderers, people who were the greatest criminals in history.

Lenin called the media who supported him "useful idiots." In that respect he described them correctly. He said that the communist revolution would only succeed because it had useful idiots in the West who would support it. He himself knew that they were idiots because they didn't support it out of real intellectual conviction but because they were swept away by the propaganda of the communist revolution. Now, useful idiots you have everywhere. And you have now, today, a lot of useful idiots serving the PLO and serving other extremist, ruthless Arab regimes, and here I think the adjectives fit. You have lots of those around the world today. As a matter of fact, it seems to me like there is a certain need for this kind of ideology among the media people. And when they are deprived of the communist heroes who are by now not only passé, but totally discredited (I mean nobody can take Fidel Castro seriously any more; it's become a farce), they must have other heroes so they have a hero like Arafat and other persons who would fit the description that Castro would fit. So, it's not unlikely that such descriptions of Sharon and others would occur.

But there is also another slightly more benevolent, certainly more benign explanation. And that is, this is a very difficult conflict. I think anyone who knows anything about this area knows that it's as difficult as the conflict with the Irish. The Irish conflict has been going on for hundreds of years, and it doesn't look like it's close to a solution, even now in this modern age when everybody wants it to become solvable. This is a very difficult conflict and the West wants it resolved — as we do, of course. Everybody wants this resolved. And it's very difficult to resolve it as long as you have dictatorships on one side and a democracy on the other, because dictatorships are not bound by anything. They don't have a parliament in which their policies are debated. They don't have a free press in which leaders are criticized. They don't have to give an accounting to anyone. So, if a dictator wants to continue a state of war even if it costs him a million of his citizens, as one dictator said, "You continue it." All of this means that if the Western mediating partners, like the United States, want to promote a compromise between a dictatorship and a democracy, they exert the same kind of pressure on both to start with. You know, pressing one . . . go ahead and compromise a little bit. And the other one . . . go ahead and compromise a little bit.

There's one big difference — the dictator doesn't have to compromise because he doesn't have to worry about anybody in his country causing him trouble if he doesn't compromise. Nor does he have to worry about the extent of the casualties which might be caused by his not compromising. Everybody was talking about it very recently when the bombing of Iraq came up. Everybody took it for granted that if you killed a hundred thousand Iraqis in this bombing, and obviously every effort was going to be made not to kill anyone, but even if you killed a hundred thousand Iraqis, everybody took it for granted that Saddam Hussein wouldn't care. Even a man like Sadat who was generally was a man who wanted peace in this area said, "I don't care if it costs me a million Egyptian lives, I'm going to do this and that, and I'm going to attack Israel."

So this is the kind of talk you never hear in a democracy for a simple reason — no democratic leader can get away with it. If the United States wants to press on both sides, and it presses one and sees that there is absolutely no movement there because of dictatorship (and that applies to Arafat, too, because he's a dictator), it looks for the path of less resistance. In this case the less resistance is the democracy. A democracy you can pressure, because in a democracy, first of all, the press is extremely critical, in particular in this case in Israel where the press is always more critical of the right-wing government than it is of the left-wing government. And it has a parliament it has to answer to. There is a change of government possible if you don't do what the people expect you to do. If you express willingness to sacrifice lives, you are ostracized from the word "go." These things make it very difficult for a democracy to resist the pressure of a superpower like the United States, and that is why they say if Israel wants it, we can have peace. Of course; if Israel withdraws, if Israel makes concessions, if Israel decides to fold, we'll have peace. By the way, they're wrong in that, too. Because that is the essential, the quintessential, I should say, appeasement policy — when you beat up on your friends and you reward your enemies because you think that will bring about stability and peace.

This is what happened in the '30s. We are not facing here a Nazi empire, or a Nazi, or even an emergent Nazi state, but the same principle always applies between dictatorships and democracies. And the tendency of the superpowers of those days, which were Britain and France, was to pacify Germany by pressing on their friend, a democracy, rather than pressing on a dictatorship, Germany, because they knew it was useless. Hitler could say "no," and it wouldn't make any difference. Nobody would do anything to him if he continued with his outrageous attitude. The same thing is happening today and that is why we must muster all our forces, all our faith, and all our friends here and abroad to help us resist this kind of pressure.

Jim Fletcher: Mr. Arafat has made a lot of noise about declaring a Palestinian state. What would be the Israeli response to something like that?

David Bar-Illan: We can't prevent him from declaring a state, I presume. I don't think it will be very smart of him to do it because a state can only declare sovereignty over areas of the territory that it controls and there isn't very much of it at this point. As you know, 98 percent of the Palestinian people in this country are ruled by Palestinians. They're under the Palestinian National Authority. There's no more what they would call an occupation. Their lives are ruled by the Palestinian National Authority. They have their own government, their own legislature, their own court system — it's all within the framework of a dictatorship, but it's theirs. They have their own armed forces, they have their own flag, they have their own representations abroad, and they are recognized by the international community. They have practically all the components, all of the ingredients, all the trappings of a state. They don't have yet, and I hope they never will have, the ability to raise a very large army — especially one equipped with heavy weapons. They have an armed force of about 50,000, which is very large for the number of the population, but they aren't able to achieve their objectives because we are still controlling the borders; they are not able to import tanks and airplanes and big cannons and that sort of thing. If they do declare a state, I imagine that most of the world will recognize it, perhaps even the United States. I don't know. We will fight against it as much as we can for the simple reason that a sovereign state can do precisely the things that I said they don't do now. And that is, raise a very large army, equip it with heavy weapons, which would be extremely dangerous being across the street from us, and form alliances with radical regimes whose declared purpose is to destroy the state of Israel.

Think for a minute of what would have happened now

that you've seen those demonstrations in favor of Saddam Hussein organized by the Palestinian National Authority, demonstrations which called for the destruction of Israel, which called upon Saddam Hussein to bring in the chemicals to wipe out Tel Aviv and other cities.

Think of (and of course we have seen these demonstrations and as you know they burn not only the Israeli flag, but also the American flag) that sentiment in a sovereign state which is able to do what it wants. They certainly could form an alliance with Iraq, with Saddam Hussein. It could bring in overnight 50 thousand volunteers, 100 thousand, 150 thousand, whatever. We would have to stop it because that already poses an existential danger to the state of Israel. It is no longer just the guerrilla warfare that they can wage against us, but something much more serious. They could bring the Iraqi or Iranian Air Force right into their airports. It seems like nothing could stop them once they're sovereign, but we would have to stop it, obviously, because we wouldn't be able to allow this kind of danger to be at our doorstep. It would start hostilities. That's not what you want around here. So, it's not a very promising prospect to have a Palestinian state here and that is why we will try to do whatever we can to prevent its establishment, to prevent it from becoming a fully sovereign entity which can do all the things I enumerated.

Jim Fletcher: What do U.N. resolutions 242 and 338 actually require of Israel?

David Bar-Illan: People always misunderstand these resolutions, but again partly because of the success of Arab propaganda to impart the impression that it means that we have to withdraw from all the territories that were won in the 1967 war — which was, after all, a war of aggression against us. It doesn't say anything of the sort. It says that Israel must withdraw from territories taken in 1967. It doesn't say *all* the territories, just territories.

This has been reiterated over and over again by the

people who wrote the resolution. After all, it's not an ancient document. It's a document from 1967. And that means that having already withdrawn from 91 percent of the territories, we don't really have to withdraw from any more, because that would certainly meet their requirement of withdrawing from territories. But what I think should be noticed even more is that Israel must have "recognized and secure borders."

Secure borders mean that returning to the '67 lines (which is what most Arabs interpret this to mean) is, of course, nonsense because no one could claim, not in his wildest dreams or nightmares, that those lines were secure borders. You can look at this type of map and you can understand that it actually requires that we have not only the Golan Heights, but much of Judea and Samaria (known as the West Bank) and a lot of other territory in order to make ourselves secure.

Jim Fletcher: In one of your columns you describe blatant anti-Semitism as hating Jews more than is absolutely necessary.

David Bar-Illan: I quoted the British as saying: "An anti-Semite is one who hates Jews more than is absolutely necessary." It's sort of a British — I wouldn't say a joke — a kind of a saying.

Jim Fletcher: Do you see anti-Semitism as a worse problem? Do you have any reason for optimism? Where do you see it going?

David Bar-Illan: I'm afraid I'm becoming less and less optimistic about it. I think that individual anti-Semitism, that is anti-Semitism against individual Jews as such, is definitely on the wane and especially in America. I really think that it is a disappearing phenomenon in America. It may exist among some neo-Nazi groups and among some very militant black groups, as represented by somebody like Louis Farrakhan and people like that. But that's on the wane I believe. What has taken its place, as I referred to before, is anti-Zionism and anti-Israelism — that is, treating the whole nation of the Jews, that is the nation of Israel, differently from the way you treat any other nation. That is really the expression of today's anti-Semitism. This is today more the channel into which anti-Semitic passions seem to be drawn.

David Lewis: Since the end result of the channeled anti-Semitism into Israel is so demonic in its desires, it actually means that they want to destroy Israel totally and hence cripple the Jewish people in the world forever. I don't think that land for peace is going to ever satisfy the Arabs.

David Bar-Illan: Well, we don't have any doubt about that. We don't have doubt about satisfying them.

David Lewis: Until there is one Jewish ghetto left in Haifa. They still can't tolerate it because it's there, just because it's there.

David Bar-Illan: We don't kid ourselves about that. I don't think anything will satisfy them. We're trying to reach some kind of a, let's say, modus vivendi — a peaceful kind of coexistence by making our borders defensible. But we're not for one minute kidding ourselves that a [false] peace treaty as differentiated from a real peace treaty can substitute for defensible, defendable, secured borders. There is no substitute for those for the time being. You can have a non-defendable border between the United States and Canada. You can have them between Holland and Belgium. You cannot have them between us and the Palestinians. And that is perhaps the main misconception, I think, of the Oslo agreement, if that is indeed what the architects of the Oslo agreement had in mind. But it is nowhere in the Oslo agreement that we have to go back to the '67 lines or something like that. So that's why we say we are perfectly willing to live by the Oslo agreement, providing that the Palestinians live by them too and do what they're supposed to do. But as such the Oslo agreements don't call for any specific withdrawals to any specific lines. So we can decide that in the frame of status talks.

David Lewis: Well, David, we're going to do everything in our power to defend you.

David Bar-Illan: Well, thank you very much. As I said before, it is because of this hostility and antagonism that seems to permeate in the world that we really have to muster all the forces that we can and that we have. We have to hope for the kind of support that we have been getting from our friends and without which we can't really survive. I don't have to tell you what the array of forces is. We have 5 million Jews in this country and the Arab world today consists of 250 million Arabs . . . add another 700 to 800 million Moslems, most of whom, by the way, are not particularly hostile as such, but if it came to an armed conflict they would have no choice but to side with the anti-Israel forces. So we must have all the help we can get, especially in the United States, because, after all, that is really the only superpower today. It may not be that way in about 10 to 15 years, it could change, but for the time being, it is certainly the only superpower and certainly the only military superpower in practical terms which one can rely on today. So any help we can get in that respect, of course, is of vital importance to us.

David Lewis: Do you have any final words you'd like to address to the American Christian community?

David Bar-Illan: I think what I've said now about faith and trust and loyalty really applies to our relationship with the evangelical community in particular that supports the rightness of Israel's cause, the justice of our being here. And that's really what is so important.

I'd like to refer to an editorial by Charles Krauthammer that appeared in the *Washington Post*. Because there he really touches on what the problem is here, which very few people seem to understand. On the very first day that the Oslo agreement was signed on the White House lawn by the late Yitzhak Rabin and Yasser Arafat, Arafat gave a talk to the Palestinian people on Jordanian television in which he said that this was just the first step in the plan of phases for the destruction of Israel. Of course he didn't say "plan of phases for the destruction of Israel," because it was enough for him to say the 1974 Rabat plan, which everybody knows is that plan.

He said again just a few weeks ago, on the first of the year, which is the anniversary of the establishment of the Fatah movement in 1964, that anybody who complains about a peace process shouldn't, because this is just the first phase, you know, this is what we are doing here. Think of that and of this tremendous outpouring of sympathy — organized demonstrations by the Palestinian Authority in favor of Saddam Hussein, calling for what Krauthammer had rightly called the genocide of the Jews of Israel, because they call, "Bring the chemicals, and bomb Tel Aviv, and destroy Tel Aviv!" When you see that on the maps of the Palestinian Authority the word "Israel" doesn't appear and Palestine covers everything from the Jordan to the Mediterranean. When you see textbooks in which the Arabic language lessons for the fifth grade do not even include anything of religion or philosophy (we're talking about fifth grade language studies, like parts of sentences, and the sentence says the Jews must be kicked out of this country); when you see this constant brainwashing which extends from kindergarten to university — when you see all this, you really have to understand the dimensions of this problem.

Because there is absolutely not a glimpse of a desire on the side of the Palestinians in particular, maybe even the Arabs in general, with very few exceptions, to really make peace, to direct the whole point of view towards peace and acceptance of Israel here. Then you really wonder how it can progress unless we make a change in this direction.

If I'm optimistic at all, it's because I know there are layers in Palestinian society, especially the middle class, which really want peace with Israel. Whether or not the middle class will be able to make itself known and affect the direction of the Palestinian government in such a way that it will really go in the direction of peace is the $64,000 question. Now if that doesn't happen we will not have peace, and if it does, we will. But for the time being, the signs are not particularly encouraging.

David Lewis: Unfortunately.

David Bar-Illan: Yes, well, look David . . . I keep being optimistic mainly because in the Middle East you can live here without being optimistic, and I keep telling myself if even ten years ago anyone would have said that the communist empire was about to collapse and that democracy, or at least a quasi-democracy kind of order, would take over in eastern Europe — he would have been considered a madman, a hopeless dreamer. Nevertheless, it happened. I'm not saying that the constellation of forces and the kind of powers that exist in this region give room for such predictions to be made easily, but nobody expected it in the Soviet Empire, either. So maybe we'll be lucky. Maybe something will happen.

The fact is that the earth has turned into a global village and the message of the West inevitably reaches the Middle East and there's no way you can keep a nation or society closed anymore. All it requires is an antenna for anybody to catch anything he wants from the whole world. Which is, by the way, why Iran couldn't keep the population down. It has not come out in any kind of real liberation, but the vote for Khatami (although Khatami himself is unable to do anything about it for the time being) was 75 percent. It is a show of a tremendous passion against the rule of the Ayatollahs and that shouldn't be underestimated. And it all comes from the connection to the outside world. They tell me that when you board a plane leaving the

Tehran airport, the minute the wheels leave the ground, all the women lift their chadors, and the little walkmans and radios come out, Western music suddenly permeates the planc, women take out lipstick and start putting it on. It's that kind of rebellion that starts occurring the minute the plane is in the air. And it shows a certain desire to get away from the oppression of the fundamentalist regime there. And I can't imagine that it will be possible to resist this kind of passion for very long.

David Lewis: Well, David, we're not quitters.

David Bar-Illan: I know you're not.

David Lewis: We'll fight on until we've got the victory.

YEHUDA LEVY

Journalist, IDF officer

Seated in the lobby of Tel Aviv's Dan Hotel, we waited for a dear and respected friend. Yehuda, a top journalist in Israel for years, also shares the Zionist world view and gave us remarkable insights into the media's role in Middle East coverage.

Yehuda Levy

Tragically, just when Israel needed his perspective and insight, Yehuda suffered a massive, fatal heart attack in 1999. After serving as publisher of the *Jerusalem Post*, he had launched a new publishing venture in order to bring a balanced view to the table of Middle East negotiations. His son, Rani, is a young politician on the rise in Israel.

David Lewis: Yehuda, I understand that you've launched a new Hebrew language newspaper, and I understand that you've gotten a very strong, positive response.

Yehuda Levy: I don't need to tell you, David, that most of the media here unfortunately is a sort of liberal biased media.

David Lewis: Liberal, left-wing socialists.

Yehuda Levy: Right. They forgot all about their Zionist values, even Jewish values, and we decided that a new newspaper should come to exist in which Jewish and Zionist values would be dominating the paper. Also, no less important is the fact that this newspaper proclaims itself to be, and it is, a "clean" newspaper. Namely, not a yellow tabloid like a couple of the bigger newspapers in this country here. Clean of pornography, clean of unethical language, and unethical journalistic base altogether. And so much . . . it proves that the potential is really there.

So hopefully between now and the end of this year we will increase the circulation up to around 35,000. We are increasing by about 100 new subscribers every day.

David Lewis: That's a good report.

Yehuda Levy: And by the end of this year, God willing, we'll move into a daily.

David Lewis: Good. By the way, Mr. Fletcher is the editor-in-chief of New Leaf Press, a book publishing house which sends millions of books around the world continuously.

Yehuda Levy: Very good.

David Lewis: We're here to gather information for a new book about Israel. It's going to be designed for the broadest market possible and should allow people like you to tell Israel's story from your heart and your mind, and get beyond the bias of the leftist press in America for example.

Yehuda Levy: And the leftist press of Israel, too.

David Lewis: Yes . . . well, I can understand the leftist press of America.

Yehuda Levy: You do?

David Lewis: I understand where they're coming from, but I just don't comprehend why the Israeli press has become so suicidal.

Yehuda Levy: Yeah.

David Lewis: It's a *balagan gadol* [a big confusion]. What's the problem?

Yehuda Levy: To tell you the truth, I am more in a position to understand the leftist press in America than I can understand the leftist press in Israel.

David Lewis: That's what I mean.

Yehuda Levy: Oh, that's what you said. I'm sorry. So we think alike. I'm glad, because as I tried to explain to Jim Fletcher a few minutes earlier, I believe that what happened here in the last 20 years or so, is that we have seen a centralization of all the leftist-liberal ideas, liberal in the negative sense of it. They are trying to become part of the bigger, global village, and forget all the uniqueness of the state of Israel and the Jewish people in itself.

David Lewis: Absolutely. You're right about that.

Yehuda Levy: While doing all this, they forget about those Zionist roots, their Jewish roots. They want to become like all the others. They imitate others, and in a reverse circle, the others imitate them. So I say, the press in America, for instance, is quite a bit influenced by the press in Israel and vice versa, which makes the situation much worse.

The press, sometime after the Yom Kippur War, and many of us feel because of the trauma the Israelis went through in this war, decided (or without making a decision) to just sacrifice almost every sacred value. And it became worse during the Galilee operation, and the war in Lebanon in 1982, during which I was the military spokesman of the IDF in Beirut for many months. I've seen how our journalists made a tremendous effort to justify almost everything the other side did and claimed, rather than try and stand with the side that they were supposed to serve.

I'm not saying that the media's task is to be the mouthpiece of its government, this is not exactly what I mean. . . .

David Lewis: But not to attack all the values of the nation.

Yehuda Levy: Not to attack all the values, not to seek. . . .

David Lewis: They even try to revise history to suit their own views.

Yehuda Levy: That's right, and taking for granted almost everything that the other side, the enemy, says. That is becoming worse and worse by the year. It has to do with the rise of the Likud to control most of the governments since 1977. These guys found themselves in a heaven in their lives. They can be strong opposition to the government and criticize it. I saw this in a dramatic way when I entered the *Jerusalem Post* ten years ago. It was unbelievable what I saw there. How Jewish Israeli journalists wrote day by day, almost everything against the ideas, against the government, and for the Palestinians, for the intifada, for the values of the other side — as if everything the other side does is justified.

David Lewis: But in your stay with the *Jerusalem Post*, you turned that around.

Yehuda Levy: Oh, yes, within a few months I put an end to this. First of all, I've introduced what I believe are real journalistic standards in which, without being extreme in either direction, we hit a moderation that actually represented reality and the truth. And more than that, first of all, I demanded that reporting news would be reporting news, and not mixed with biased personal opinions. So we have separated totally in the *Post*, immediately after I came in, the news reporting as factual, as close to the truth as possible, and separated it totally from commentary, from opinion, etc. And when introducing opinion and commentary, it was balanced as you say. It reflected the entire rainbow of the Israeli society and not just the one-sided or biased opinion as it used to until that time. And therefore the *Post* since then has gained very high respect all over the world and has become a very influential newspaper until this very day.

David Lewis: What was the circulation of the *Post* when you left?

Yehuda Levy: You'll have to divide it between the circulation of the daily newspaper here and the weekly international edition, which circulates all over the world. If we're talking about the daily here, on the weekends when I left, the circulation was close to 50,000 and you have to remember that Israel is a Hebrew-speaking country and, in fact, the 50,000 would represent almost 95 percent of the potential readers of the English language in this country. And during the weekdays, it was 25-26,000.

The international edition of the *Jerusalem Post* circulated all over the world is close to 100,000 out of which, 55,000 is in North America. But it reaches all the corners of the globe, you know, from Papua, New Guinea to South America, etc.

David Lewis: What is the editorial slant now in the *Jerusalem Post*?

Yehuda Levy: Well, I want to believe that it remained more or less as I left it a year ago, but now I'm not sure about that, because I'm hearing some complaints about some changes, about some drifts that took place to the left. When I speak to the guy who replaced me, he believes that he has made it more of a centralist newspaper.

David Lewis: What's his name?

Yehuda Levy: Norman Spector. Norman Spector used to be the Canadian Ambassador to Israel until five years ago. And he is now the publisher of the *Jerusalem Post*.

David Lewis: Who took David Bar-Illan's place?

Yehuda Levy: Well, when David Bar-Illan left our paper, I appointed Jeff Barak — he's number two.

David Lewis: Barak?

Yehuda Levy: Jeff Barak, as the editor. But, knowing these two guys, I cannot say that I can automatically blame any of these for being leftists or anything like that, but maybe their control of the material is not as tight as mine was. So that's the only way I can explain.

David Lewis: Who owns the *Post*?

Yehuda Levy: The owner of the *Post* is a Canadian company named Hollinger which has over 650 newspapers and other publications all over the world, including the *Chicago Sun Times*, the *London Daily Telegraph*, and many, many others. But I can tell you that in my eight and a half years, they really granted me a total freedom to run the *Post* in the way I saw fit. So, hopefully, the *Post* will continue to be an influential and a very balanced and good newspaper. I hope it will.

David Lewis: I miss Bar-Illan's column "Eye on the Media."

Yehuda Levy: Right. That was a great column.

David Lewis: That will go down in history as one of the great series of significant essays.

Yehuah Levy: I'm planning in my weekly newspaper to introduce such a column. We are going to start this in about three to four weeks from now. Every week there will be such a column, similar to the "Eye on the Media."

David Lewis: Might I suggest that at some time in the future, however far down the road this is, you might think of making an English language translation of your paper and publishing it, too.

Yehuda Levy: Yes, I've already had such requests from many of my friends in the United States and I will certainly plan this in the near future. I cannot tell exactly when it will happen, but we will certainly have to do it, if we really want to be influential and give the readers a different angle from a credible, conservative Israeli media, we really have to reach English-speaking or English-reading people.

Jim Fletcher: With regard to bias among the Israeli press, the left wing, do you think that is simply a case of naiveté when it comes to the PLO and the peace process or is it something more sinister?

Yehuda Levy: I believe that it comes from a basis of naiveté, because I know many of these journalists that we are speaking about and I don't suspect any one of them to be a traitor intentionally. I believe that, in the depths of their hearts, they want the good of this country and the good of this nation, the same as I do. But it started with naiveté and it drifted on to becoming, as I explained earlier, a part of the global journalistic elite which unfortunately is holding this leftist view wherever they are, whether it's in the States or here or somewhere in Europe. No matter where you examine this phenomenon you come to the same conclusions.

So, I'll give you some examples of the latest expressions. As you know, our prime minister, Benjamin Netanyahu, has been the target of vicious attacks by the Israeli media since day one. They didn't really give him even one day to let him get used to the fact that he was the prime minister of this nation. And let me tell you that this man, I believe, has the most difficult task of any prime minister on this earth. There is no other head of state in this world that has such a complex, responsible duty as Bibi Netanyahu has. And they didn't give him the slightest chance and attacked him over everything.

Yes, he made mistakes, because first of all , he lacked the experience. He never was a prime minister before. He never even managed any big organization of any kind and certainly such a man has to have some time to get used to his position and to learn. If I judge Bibi's behavior and functioning all together today compared to the first 6 or even 12 months, there is a huge difference. He has learned for sure. And I myself criticized him for many of the mistakes he made. There were good enough reasons for criticism, yes. But that is not the point at all. Almost everything he did, whether wrong or right, was automatically criticized and attacked viciously by almost the entire Israeli media.

A month or two ago, one leftist journalist of an important newspaper here, *Ha'aretz* — the journalist's name is Ari Shavit, who is known as a leftist journalist, per se — published an article one weekend that ran over eight pages, in which he went out of his way to explain why leftist journalists love to hate Bibi Netanyahu.

Jim Fletcher: The year of hating Bibi.

Yehuda Levy: Yes, that's the *year of hating Bibi.* And you would have thought that would give a second thought to the intelligent people who run the Israeli media. But it was a symbol, a cause célèbre in this whole performance of the Israeli media. Since then, the other journalists or the other media tried to analyze why did he write what he wrote from different angles. Rather than to take into consideration the facts that he touched and the analysis that he made, they wanted to see what was wrong with the guy that could have written things like that about the Prime Minister of Israel. It's very disturbing. I can tell you another thing. Edor Netanyahu, Bibi's brother, is a doctor. Edor Netanyahu has just published a book named *Itamar K.* Itamar is a popular Hebrew name, and "K" stands for the first letter of his surname. This is a book that is very cynical and very critical of the entire cultural-journalistic elite of the state of Israel.

David Lewis: Is the book in Hebrew only, or is it also available in English?

Yehuda Levy: It's in Hebrew. I don't really know if he intends to translate into English. I hope he does. In fact, in this week's issue that comes out tomorrow to the market, there is a big interview with him over the book and in general as well. Beyond reason of journalistic behavior and the fact that they side automatically with what CNN says or with what Yassar Arafat says, without difference between the two, is not necessarily good journalism performance.

David Lewis: Now, in the American media, we constantly read outright lies, not just mistakes, not just interpretations. For example, the rioting in the streets of Har Homa, as reported on American TV news, showed footage of the riot, television pictures that turned out to be riots that took place seven years earlier in Gaza. There are no streets of Har Homa to be rioting on.

Then there is the distorted reporting of Israel's opening of the ancient Hasmonean tunnel by the Western Wall. Over and over, they said the tunnel was being dug under the Temple Mount undermining the Al-Aqsa Mosque, ignoring the fact that the tunnel was not under the Temple Mount and nowhere near the Al-Aqsa Mosque nor the Dome of the Rock.

No one in the media bothered to mention that there was an agreement between the Wakf [Moslem religious authority] and the Israeli government that there would be a two-fold exchange of privilege — one being the opening of the tunnel, which was the Hasmonean tunnel of over 2,000 years in age, not something newly dug. And in exchange, the Moslems would be able to open a mosque in the Stables of Solomon.

Yehuda Levy: You're right, David. This is one specific example that you're giving, but I can tell you that it is happening almost every day in the general, so-called attitude to the so-called peace process.

David Lewis: Yehuda, what do you ascribe this to as far as the American journalists are concerned? Are they just mistaken, are they naive, or just stupid?

Yehuda Levy: They are not stupid. They are not naive.

David Lewis: Do you think it is deliberate deception?

Yehuda Levy: It is a deliberate deception.

David Lewis: I believe that. I believe it has its roots in anti-Semitism.

Yehuda Levy: I hear and I see quite often this Mr. Walter Rogers of the CNN who sits here in Jerusalem and how he reports events or developments of all kinds in which the government or Bibi himself are involved, and always, automatically he represents the Palestinian side. He doesn't even make any effort to hide that, and it's unbelievable the way they are doing it. It's not only him, it's the others, too. I haven't seen him or any other serious journalist who stands against Yasser Arafat or one of his senior aides, and really asks them the tough questions when talking about why the so-called peace process is stuck. Israel is automatically blamed. No one asks him, Arafat or his senior aide, "What about the constant violations?" And there is a whole list that these journalists are very familiar with, of Palestinian violations of the Oslo agreement, of the Hebron agreement, signed and backed by the United States by Warren Christopher and Dennis Ross. No one asks them the question. It's unpleasant. It's unpolite.

David Lewis: It's no longer polite to be anti-Semitic, but it's very polite to be anti-Israel or anti-Zionist.

Yehuda Levy: That's the current replacement, sure.

David Lewis: It's just a switch of terminology, but Anti-Zionism is anti-Semitism.

Yehuda Levy: That is correct. If you ask any of these guys, "Why is the peace process stuck today?" you automatically hear all the reasons that Israel is to be blamed for this. The fact that the Palestinians have done almost nothing about terrorism, about diminishing the Hamas infrastructure, about turning terrorists into the hands of Israel as it is signed and agreed. Just a couple of days ago, you were here. You heard the news about the confiscation of a huge arsenal that was smuggled from Jordan by the order of the Palestinian Authority. It was not just an act of some criminals. The chief of the Palestinian police himself was involved in terror. He himself ordered terror activities

THE LAST WAR

against Israel. They are arming themselves beyond any proportion that is mentioned in the Oslo agreement, let alone their failure. It's not just a failure. It's by intention they don't do it. It is not a mere oversight that they refuse to correct, to amend the Palestinian Covenant. The list is long, and I must admit, to my horror, that I cannot say it only about Walter Rogers or other American journalists; it's true about Israeli journalists as well. It's really a shame. It's even frightening.

Jim Fletcher: Well, we get a trickle of information in the West, such as a columnist will report that at Arafat's headquarters in Gaza, his maps on the walls make no reference to Israel. That is a chilling fact, yet it is not reported widely in the media.

Yehuda Levy: It goes much beyond that. If you examine the entire culture of the Palestinian people of today, of the post-Oslo agreement, check their kindergardens, their schools, their mosques, there is a continuous instigation of hatred toward Israel. You would have expected this side, if it really means peace, to start educating at least its youth, forget the old generation that was involved in terror action against Israel, because it is hard to change what's in their hearts. You'd have expected them to start at least a sort of education towards peace. Not only does it not exist, but the opposite exists. The hatred that they pour into the hearts of their children is frightening.

And you say to yourself, with all the official discussions and agreement, *If this doesn't change, nothing will help. I mean, no piece of paper will help us live in peace if the other side thinks and feels that the Jews are to be hated, the Jews are a target for terror activities, their suicide bombers are the heroes.* What can you expect to happen — let alone now — but in 10, 20, or 50 years from now? Their books, their textbooks, their speeches in the mosques, the explanations of their teachers, and what they hear from their number one chief, Yassar Arafat. . .

Jim Fletcher: Which are themselves blatant violations of Oslo.

Yehuda Levy: That's right. That's right.

David Lewis: Do the Western journalists understand this Moslem mentality as a threat?

Yehuda Levy: They don't. They don't, and that's part of the problem. It's not only the journalists, let me tell you. I'm afraid it starts with your then president Clinton, going down to the last man or woman who deals with any issue concerning the Moslem world. They do not understand the mentality. They do not want to think that in this part of the world things work differently, that mentality and philosophy are totally different. What is correct or true in North America or in Europe is not correct and true here. You have to take into consideration that it goes far beyond the immediate problem between us and the Palestinians. It goes to the problem of Saddam Hussein, of Iran, of Iraq, of Syria.

Unfortunately, we are perceived as somehow being different in this part of the world. Israel is going to be the number one target of these mistakes that the leaders of the world are now making.

Suicide bomber in Jerusalem, September 1997.

David Lewis: Well, it's the jihad mentality, that's for sure. I don't think that our Western politicians or the journalists understand this. You cannot rationalize with people who have a radical mindset. There's no changing a rationality.

Yehuda Levy: It's the jihad mentality and it's more than that. They don't understand one very basic issue — the conflict here in this piece of land, eretz Israel, the land of Israel, is not over a few inches of land or a few square miles of land in the West Bank or anywhere else — it's a conflict between two religions, between two mentalities.

David Lewis: It's a spiritual warfare.

Yehuda Levy: It's a spiritual war, for sure. Even if we gave them all of the West Bank, as the late Rabin had probably planned to do, I do not believe that we would have had peace by now or in ten years from now. And that is because there was the one step and after the one step there is another one, and they've gone a few steps forward already, no doubt. And I don't want to be inside the Gaza Strip or in Nablus, I don't need to be in the midst of these places. I know very well that if I let them go another step, then we'll be under pressure to go another step, and another step, until there would be no state of Israel. There is no doubt in this respect.

David Lewis: That part of the covenant never really gets changed.

Yehuda Levy: Of course, of course. Otherwise how can they justify to their people the whole concept? And unfortunately it has some side effects on other very worrying matters here. For example, take the Israeli Arabs, including the Israeli Bedouins in the Negev. The more they see that the Palestinian entity is rising and flourishing and getting more or less what it wishes to get, they start to ask themselves, why should we be loyal to the state of Israel? Why not totally side with our people, the Palestinians? They would not have said such a thing 15 years ago. So the Oslo agreement is bad in many aspects, but this is one more that not many people think about. It shook the entire Zionist foundation of the state of Israel.

David Lewis: Was Yossi Beilin the architect of Oslo?

Yehuda Levy: Sure, yes, but you have to give him credit that he was then part of the government and he had the full backing of Shimon Peres as the minister of foreign affairs, who in a later stage managed to get Prime Minister Rabin to go along with this whole thing. It started by unofficial negotiations in Oslo or in other parts of Europe by four unprofessional guys, some of whom do not understand the defense, security, or even geography of Israel. They understand almost nothing about the mentality of the Arabs, as we just mentioned earlier, and they brought a more or less cooked deal to Beilin and from Beilin to Shimon Peres. It is as if they had decided that the end of the days have come at last and the Messiah is coming, and there is a new Middle East. And they started to get carried away with these dreams. Again, I'm saying I don't suspect any of them of really wishing bad to the state of Israel.

David Lewis: I'm not so sure.

Yehuda Levy: Well, I'm sure. I'm sure. They are not traitors — at least they did not mean to be.

David Lewis: Oh, you mean the Israelis involved?

Yehuda Levy: The Israelis, that's what I'm saying. The Israelis who along with Shimon Peres to the last guy who negotiated in Oslo did not mean to achieve any threat to the existence of the state of Israel. They believed they were doing the right thing and that they were bringing us the peace that we have all dreamed about for many years, but they did it in such an amateurish way.

David Lewis: It would have been wonderful if the Arabs had cooperated.

Yehuda Levy: Yes, of course. Who doesn't want peace? Everyone in this country is dreaming of peace for sure.

David Lewis: Is it true that Beilin and Peres had secret meetings with the Oslo people before they told Rabin about it? So they cooked it up and handed it to him on a platter.

Yehuda Levy: Well, I would say this very carefully. In the very beginning, he knew nothing. Certainly in the second stage, he knew that there were some contacts and some talks to try and see if there was any way of reaching anything. On the third stage, he got something already finished and finalized that he had to approve. And then he had the conflict — to become the one who resists an opportunity of achieving peace with the Palestinians.

So here was Shimon Peres, the architect of this whole thing, and he [Rabin], the prime minister, had to decide whether he's dismissing it on the face of it or going along with it. Dismissing it means that he would be the one who would go down in history as the one who killed the opportunity as it looked in the eyes of those who made it, of course, the opportunity for achieving peace. So he started to go along with it, very hesitating, very carefully, very reluctantly and many hesitations. As he proceeded he became more and more convinced that he should take the risk. Unfortunately, by doing this, he also made half of the nation his enemy. He had forgotten that he could not present such a solution to the Knesset in which he didn't have the majority except with the Arab votes (the Israeli members of the Knesset who are Arabs and automatically sided with the Palestinian side, of course). So, in fact, he did not represent the Jewish majority in this country and he ignored that totally.

When he was criticized, in turn he started to attack. He attacked the settlers on the Golan, he attacked settlers in Judea and Samaria, and he attacked everyone who said anything critical.

David Lewis: And yet he had a great hand in starting the settlement movement.

Yehuda Levy: Yes, that's right.

David Lewis: He just turned right around. He surprised the Americans.

Yehuda Levy: He surprised Washington for sure.

David Lewis: Thank you, Yehuda.

RA'ANAN LEVY

Member, Third Way Party

Recently, while in Israel, I had the opportunity to conduct a round table discussion on many subjects such as the Golan Heights and other issues concerning Israel's security and safe future. Participating in this discussion were Thomas Brimmer, Ra'anan (Rani) Levy, Jim Fletcher, Avigdor Rosenberg, and myself, David Lewis,.

David Lewis: Rani, why do you think the media is so biased against Israel, just in general?

Ra'anan Levy

Rani Levy: I don't know why they are, but I think there is no argument any more that they aren't. Israel's major problem today, I think, is the media, the shallowness in which the events in Israel are being covered. The attempt to go around the world in 30 minutes — it's ridiculous, and is continuously harming Israel. It is hurting our ability to explain the real issues, the truth, the complexity of the problems, and I think it will never change. It is a reality that Israel has to live with and to constantly fight the media, and to try and mobilize the truth, as we see it, to the world. We could do very little to change the situation.

Tom Brimmer: I'd like to suggest that there are some legitimate reasons why the media takes an anti-Israel stance. One of them is terror. The newsman who goes out there and covers the story and takes a pro-Israel stance has placed his very life in danger. The newsman who takes a pro-Israel source may never have that source available to him again. In other words, simply put, the news media is based on survival and the survival to some degree is based on taking a stance against Israel. That's a fact, that's reality, that's hard.

It's something that's very difficult for the media themselves to deal with. They are not being adequately protected from terror. They are being infiltrated by terror and they are being influenced by huge amounts of money from outsiders who are in support of terror.

David Lewis: Any comment on that?

Rani Levy: Yes, I think that to expand on what Tom said, Israel is also a place that is truly a haven for journalists because you can walk freely in Israel in rather troubled situations without any government on your back, without any censorship on what you say and how you say it. Compare it to places anywhere else in the Middle East. The media is completely controlled by the hosting country.

In Israel, that's not the case. Israel is the only country in the world that tolerates risking its own security by not controlling or monitoring or censoring any piece of information that comes out of (especially the Palestinian Authority) what's known as the territories.

David Lewis: I remember a number of years ago that there was an incident in Mecca where the Moslem extremists took over the mosque, the big Kaaba Mosque.

Tom Brimmer: The Iranians.

David Lewis: Yes. The news media coverage was very, very scanty — very little. This is a good example of control.

Rani Levy: There are numerous examples. I don't know how many people know what Egypt did in Raffa, on the Egyptian side of the city of Raffa, in '87, I believe. Three hundred Palestinians were killed in two days by Egyptian troops in '87.

The intifada actually started on the Egyptian side of Raffa, but the Egyptians took care of it in two days by killing 300 Palestinians. Who heard about it? Who even knows about it? And if the world, or the media, would have tried to pick Mubarak's head on this event he would have said, "This is none of your business, this is an internal Arab affair." We've heard those statements from the Arabs all the time. So, we don't need to be whining about it.

I accept it as another one of the difficulties that we have to face. We can live without the media. We have lived without the media for 50 years. So, we're prepared to take that another 50 years. We don't have a choice, I believe. The media, as Tom says, has a natural inclination to lean against Israel.

David Lewis: Leftist, socialist — that's the media.

Rani Levy: Yes. Liberal, anti-biblical. I can go on and on. And we won't change it. We have to live with it. We have to fight it. But we have to also accept it as a reality.

David Lewis: Talk about Hama in Syria, the slaughter of the people in Hama.

Rani Levy: Well, this is another example how a minor incident of several Sunni rebels who shot at an Alawi battalion in the city of Hama, which is a Syrian city, brought the reaction by President Assad of wiping out the whole town. Amnesty International assumes that 30 to 40,000 residents of Hama were massacred by President Assad.

David Lewis: Thirty to forty thousand?

Rani Levy: Yes. The Israeli intelligence believes that it was over 50,000. But, it may not be appropriate to use this figure. I really don't think it matters for the purpose of our conversation. The issue is not whether President Assad massacred 30,000 or 50,000 Syrians, the fact that counts here is that three Syrian soldiers that were killed by the Sunni rebels in Hama has brought the reaction of the destruction of all the city, the massacre of all of its residents, without a reaction from the international community.

David Lewis: Almost silence. . . .

Rani Levy: Or knowing about it. I don't remember CNN or ABC or anybody taking the case of Hama as a media event in itself that needed to be explored, investigated . . . nothing. And this hypocrisy — as I say, we can give endless examples. We will have to live with that. I don't accept that, don't get me wrong, but today as an Israeli, I'm at the point where I understand that this will not change and we just have to take that into account as one of the other forces that is working against us. There are many forces that are much more serious than the media.

David Lewis: But the media controls so much of public opinion, that it is a very serious situation.

Rani Levy: Absolutely.

David Lewis: The book that we're writing is about the media and Israel, and we want to tell Israel's story for her through our publishing channel, New Leaf Press, which distributes millions of books all over the world. We have mailing lists with a few thousand names, but with the book we'll be able to reach millions of people. We want to do very careful research and good documentation on all of these subjects.

Rani Levy: If you're focusing on the Israeli media, you may want to look at the rhetoric of the Israeli media during the last three months of the election campaign here in Israel in May '96. That was a classical example of how the Israeli media suffers from the same diseases that the international media suffers from . . . fanatic liberal . . . yes, definitely.

And I say that with great pain, because when I suffer from the BBC or the *New York Times* or CNN, at least its not my own people, but when I suffer from the Israel Broadcasting Authority or from an Israeli newspaper, I think we have a very serious problem.

And as an Israeli citizen, forget even my political opinions, I am saddened by the one-sided view of the Israeli media itself. We've had here a whole media participation and total, blunt, and out-in-the-open recruitment to promote and elevate Shimon Peres in the elections. There was not even a shred of fairness in the coverage of the Likud main candidates, or of Netanyahu as a legitimate leader of the Likud Party. There was, by the way (and that should interest you as Americans) brutal intervention in the campaign here by President Clinton himself.

President Clinton came here in, I believe, April '96 . . . hardly agreed to meet with Netanyahu. It was obvious to anybody that he was doing it just to save face. It was a meeting that was very short. I believe 15 or 20 minutes out of a six-day visit that he spent here holding Shimon Peres's hands, walking with him all over the country from one school to the other, and the message was clear. Clinton was participating in Shimon Peres's campaign. All the news media in Israel was participating in Shimon Peres's campaign. I really think that anybody who is intellectually honest can agree with me, regardless if he is a Peres supporter or Bibi Netanyahu supporter, the media here in Israel has done everything they could to delegitimize Netanyahu and portray Shimon Peres as the mother of all leaders, the father of all leaders, whatever. They almost gave him divine qualities for his statesmanship.

So these processes, all these powers that are working in the Israeli society and in the international arena, are very serious. They have strategic meanings. Don't think for a minute that the claims that Hafez Assad has from Israel on the Golan or that the claims that Arafat has from Israel on the West Bank — don't think for a minute that they stand by themselves. They all are fueled and fed and nourished by what they think their boundaries are by the international community.

If the international community would have been more clearly and openly siding with Israel, Hafez Assad would have accepted not having the Golan Heights, Arafat would have understood that he needs to settle for what he has achieved in the Oslo agreements, and none of them would have tried to go for more. The only reason they do try to go for more is not because of their great ideology. It's because when they make the total accumulation of the facts that they see in front of them, they believe — and many times they are correct — the hostility towards Israel in the European community, in the European Union, in the White House and the State Department. Fortunately not in the Congress and in the Senate, but often in the State Department. And the left-wing circles in Israel play a major role in their ability to make more achievements in the political process with Israel.

Tom Brimmer: I just want to point out that in defense of the media again, part of the problem and part of the reality here is that the left-wing political establishment is actively feeding the media, and is actively feeding the political process in such a way.

David Lewis: The worldwide media?

Rani Levy: Both.

Tom Brimmer: Yes. I would agree with that. To the extent that we have left-wing politicians going to the media and saying, "Go to Arafat and tell him that we will give him this. Go to Saddam and tell him that we will give him this. Go to Assad and tell him that we will give him this." It's not even very well hidden. In fact, it's not hidden at all. It's an active feeding process and the feeding comes from the political realm, feeding the . . . well, 89 percent, I think, was the percentage of the media that said they would support the left wing, according to a recent poll.

So there's an affinity here which goes far beyond ideology and is political, is economic, and reaches into the social strata of the media as well as the politicians.

Rani Levy: I just want to add that I really think the main focus of this is the way the Israeli, the average Israeli, tolerates these things — not on the behavior of the media. I almost don't have any quarrel with the media. They're doing their job in the way they understand it and I think this is one of the prices of democracy. I'm not in the position to tell the media how to operate. I don't care how they operate to the extent that I would tell them to operate differently.

My finger is pointed not at the media, but at the Israeli public opinion. That they put up with the way the media is treating us — this is my claim. The media is the media. It has to be, and I want it to be, a body that is so free and so independent that they can do whatever they do.

David Lewis: But it's so unbalanced.

Rani Levy: Let it be unbalanced. This is not what troubles me. I don't want a media that is dominated by anybody. So I'm not going to try to dominate it myself. I want a public opinion that is mature enough to give the food that the media is trying to give us, the right proportions and the overall pictures.

It is inconceivable to me that in a country like Israel anything the media would do would affect things like whether to give up the Golan Heights or not, or how Israel should react when the Palestinian Authority does not conduct their part of the agreements. My criticism is not on the media. It's on my brothers, the Israelis, the people here. I mean, one day a bus explodes and they are ready to drop all of the agreements and stop every political dialogue. Then if everything is peaceful for the next ten months and there's no big terrorist incident, they seem to be ready to give the whole store away. That is one of our big problems. This indicates the shallowness of a major segment of Israeli society.

To me, as an Israeli, the problem is with the density of the ability of the public opinion to hold itself, regardless of what the media says. Should I review my opinions every morning depending on what I read in the paper or what I see on TV, or what I see on the BBC? I have my Jewish roots here in this country. I am a 13th generation Sabra here. I am part of a society that took in millions of Jews from all over the world and made this their home. I have to know — when I say "I," I don't mean me personally, I mean "I" as part of Israeli society — we have to know, if you may, what do we want from ourselves? Where have to be our final borders? Where they should not be? Who do we need to be in political negotiations with, and who we should not be with?

I said many times on your radio programs, that I think the negotiation with Syria in its essence is not legitimate. Israel should not talk to Syria, period. It is an immoral act. A country that supports international terrorism, a country that supports international drug dealing, cannot be a partner for negotiation . . . period. And this whole game that Israel is a part of, the United States is a part of, to me it's totally unacceptable.

Why do I need the media? I need God. I need the house that I came from. I need the set of values that I was raised on. And that's where I should set my opinions — not on what I read in the paper. I read my paper. I watch the television. I see the news on TV. I read articles. I have leftist friends. I have Arab friends. I hear all the opinions in the world. I'm open to listen to them. But nobody can come one day and tell me to think this and the next day tell me to think that or if Clinton will come here and hold Peres's hand for five days and I watch that on TV then all of a sudden I'll think that Peres is a great leader — it should not work this way. Part of the problem is with the Israeli people themselves, and not entirely with the media.

David Lewis: Well, the problem is well defined. The question is, how do you undertake re-education of the people?

Rani Levy: That's a whole issue in itself. I don't know how far you want to go with going deep into the issues. I think it is primarily an educational issue.

And unfortunately, between '92 and '96, Israel was infected with an administration that was headed by Yitzhak Rabin for most of the time and later on by Shimon Peres. An administration that has made almost a deliberate decision to ruin and to destroy to the bone many of the fundamental values of Zionism.

David Lewis: That's a tragedy.

Rani Levy: Of course it's a tragedy. By the way, it has nothing to do with my opinion on what happened in November '95, obviously, but I think that this tragic event does not even have anything to do with Israeli society and its moral values. The murdering of Rabin was a monstrous act that no Israeli, no sane Israeli, accepts. I just want to say that for the record.

But back to the issue, the policies of Yitzhak Rabin, the rhetoric that came from his office for two and a half years and from all the gallery of ministers around him. Statements made like Yosef Sarid saying to the residents of the Golan Heights that they'd better begin looking for new homes in Galilee in the middle of a negotiation with Syria. Statements made by Rabin's own foreign minister, Shimon Peres, when he was on a visit in Morocco, saying that Israel decided to give all the Golan Heights to Syria because of a moral choice that Israel made. Listen to the words. Not because we decided to give the Golan Heights (according to Peres' system) due to our strong desire to make peace with Syria. We are now giving the Golan Heights because it belongs to them, according to the left.

Statements like that infiltrate to the deepest layers of Israeli society. The teenagers hear them, the soldiers hear them, the reservists hear them, the confused hear them, the spiritually weak hear them, and these are major sects in Israeli society. And how can we, as a nation, go then to our men in the army and expect them to fight for the Golan Heights when their own prime minister tells them that this is not God's land. They say it's just a piece of real estate.

David Lewis: And they say God's not in the real estate business.

Rani Levy: Yes. Yes.

David Lewis: Better read the Book of Genesis.

Rani Levy: Look, we are fighting evil forces all the time. This is not incomprehensible if you're spiritually reasonable.

David Lewis: It's spiritual warfare.

Rani Levy: To me, I don't see any difference between the media and having Syria around or a bus explode or . . . these are all a part of the system that operates against Israel. To me, God is the one who decides everything.

David Lewis: Right.

Rani Levy: God will determine the end fate of Israel, of the Zionist dream, of anything. And He has been doing that for many years. I think we need to take a deep breath and understand that the conflicts around us have been here for about 4,000 years and they will be here for at least 4,000 years more. If we will have the energy to look at the conflict around us through these eyes, you will see the biggest hope for a political solution.

One of our biggest problems, again, is ourselves. We are constantly convincing the other side that if they will persist, they will win. This needs to stop. Our enemies need to know that they can fight for the Golan Heights for 150 million more years, and it won't help them. They need to know that they can fight for Jerusalem as long they want, and it won't help them, either.

They need to understand, and if you're a leader, you have to say that. If you're ashamed to say it, you're not a leader. That Israel will sacrifice its men in order to stay alive is not something you should be ashamed to say. I don't understand how the ideal of having peace that kills you turned into a proper substitute to a no-war situation that keeps you alive. I don't know where that happened in the last ten years, but it happened. Today if you fight for your right to exist, if you're willing to take action when you're threatened, you're an anti-peacenik. But if you're willing to suffer and take 300 casualties from terrorism in two years, you're a great lover of peace. Everything became twisted around.

David Lewis: All mixed up.

Rani Levy: Only our determination to fight for our right to live here can prevent wars. We need to understand that principle. Only if we will make everybody understand that we will not hesitate to fight — we will not fight. The minute that we project an attitude that we are not willing to fight, we will have to fight. The more the other side believes that we are morally incompetent and that we are ideologically confused and that we're socially weak, the higher the chances are that they will make another attempt to take what they always wanted — and this is all of Israel. They thought that in '48. They thought that in '56. They thought it in '73. And how many more lessons do we need?

Every time the Arab world thought that the time was right to finish us off, they didn't care about any international law, any international peace-keeping force. They didn't care about America. They didn't think of anyone. They turned on their armored vehicles and they moved ahead. And it will not change. It's in their essence. You have to realize, Israel is not a natural entity in the Middle Eastern environment. We are hardly six millions Jews living here in the center of a region that consists of almost one billion Moslems. This is not a natural thing. And we have to understand that this is a complicated neighborhood that requires very, very long-term and long-lasting spiritual and ideological energies. If we won't have that, we won't be here.

Tom Brimmer: You're describing fundamentally Middle Eastern thinking which, to some degree at least, is confusing or perhaps even incomprehensible to the average American. Is there some way that you can help the average American understand the Moslem mindset, the Orthodox Jewish mindset, the secular Jewish mindset when it comes to thinking about politics and policy concerning war and truth?

Rani Levy: I will try to explain that from an American perspective, if I may. Look at the resistance and the public opinion objection to a military strike on Iraq just in the last few weeks. The media made it look as if every American is in favor of Saddam against Clinton and against a military strike on Baghdad. I have been enough times in America and I know enough Americans to know that this was a false picture. Yes, there were individuals, many maybe, but still individuals, a very small minority, very vocal, but a small minority.

That made it look as if Clinton has a very serious public opinion problem. Correct me if I'm wrong. This is a free conversation and I believe this was fundamentally false. I believe Clinton was, on this issue, majorly supported by the American people. Now for anybody who listens to what I say in between the lines this is the same situation we have here.

The "peace now" movement in Israel is a very small minority, but it's very vocal. People from the outside may think that they're running the country. They're not running the country. They were not even able to win an election two years ago and the majority of the Israeli society are Bible-believing people. The majority of the people in Israel are fundamental believers, strong believers in Israel's divine and everlasting right to exist in this land. And you've seen in May '96 what was the Israeli people's answer to a government that went astray from principle Zionist values.

As for the Moslem world, I believe we can have peace with the Arabs only when the United States of America will decide to make a moral step in its relationship with Israel. Unfortunately, and to a great extent, I blame ourselves also in that. The United States, since the days of George Shultz and Ronald Reagan, since the mid-eighties, has taken the stand of mediator between Israel and the Arab world. In the last 10–12 years the United States became less of an unconditional strategic ally of Israel and more of a mediator.

Now a mediator is someone that needs to be objective and fair towards both sides. If the United States wants to mediate between Israel and the Palestinians, if the United States wants to mediate between Israel and the Syrians, the United States needs to become an objective party. Because they need to deliver Israel to the Palestinians and they need to deliver Israel to the Syrians. This kind of relationship between Israel and the United States is totally unacceptable to me. I think the United States is wrong in doing this and I think Israel is wrong in trying to enjoy that sometimes.

We should demand that the whole free world — the European Union, and the United States of America — openly and unconditionally support Israel against the Arab world. I know it's very ambitious, and when I say that, I don't mean that in the childish sense that the United States needs to agree on everything Israel does, but I mean principally.

David Lewis: Thank you, Rani.

THE LAST WAR — A BIBLICAL VIEW OF HISTORY AND PROPHECY

The Jews constitute but one percent of the human race. It suggests a nebulous puff of stardust lost in the blaze of the Milky Way. Properly the Jew ought hardly to be heard of; but he is heard of, has always been heard of. He is as prominent on the planet as any other people. . . . He has made a marvelous fight in this world, in all the ages; and has done it with his hands tied behind him. . . . The Egyptian, the Babylonian, and the Persian rose, filled the planet with sound and splendor, then faded to dream-stuff and passed away; the Greek and the Roman followed, and made a vast noise, and they are gone; other peoples have sprung up and held their torch high for a time, but it burned out, and they sit in twilight now, or have vanished. The Jew saw them all, beat them all, and is now what he always was. . . . All things are mortal but the Jew; all other forces pass, but he remains. What is the secret of his immortality?[1]

This appendix is included in *The Last War* to put the book into an understandable context. If this information were to be excluded we might be thought to be misleading our readers. This book is *not about Armageddon*. It is about the centrality of Israel in God's intentions for this planet and all mankind. Indeed, it is a point of view not being widely declared today, if at all.

The one universal and continuous conflict of the ages is being waged on two levels, physical and spiritual. This information is extremely important because you are involved in the great war whether you realize it or not, or whether you want to be or not.

Why all of the emphasis on Israel and the Jewish people? Because it is their story. Because the Almighty began His Book with Moses, leader of Israel, in the days of the pharaoh who tried to destroy them. The book ends with the apocalyptic vision of John the Jewish Apostle, who describes in graphic terms the final defeat of evil, at the hand of Messiah, who is called the Lion of Judah.

Where does this include the Church? Pagans (Gentiles) can become a part of the commonwealth of Israel, by His grace and forgiveness of all sin (read Rom. 9,10, and 11). It can easily be demonstrated that the Lord expects His church to be defenders of His ancient people in the days of oppression and intifada.[2]

The biblical story of planet Earth is the saga of one long, long war involving God, His angelic and human subjects battling against Satan, and His evil hordes. This epic drama begins on page one of your Bible. God states His divine intention to destroy the works of the serpent, the devil (Gen. 3:15). There is actually only one universal war, and it concludes with the devil's final incarceration in the Lake of Fire (Rev. 19:20; 20:10). That takes place after the Millennium and the Great White Throne Judgment (Rev. 20:11).

There is one universal war, which began in eternity past with the rebellion of Lucifer, the devil. The universal war ends, after a last battle at the close of the Millennium (Rev. 20:7–8), with the final judgment and eternal imprisonment of Satan (Rev. 20:10).

Peace at Last

Then dawns an eternity of peace at last. War, cruelty, death, sickness, pain, and suffering will be a dim memory if finally remembered at all. No more cruelty or terrorism will be done, no more false accusations, no injustice, no prejudice, no more misunderstanding, no more lonely days or nights, for "God shall wipe away all tears from their eyes" (Rev. 21:4).

Within the scope of the one universal war there will be two planetary or earthly world wars with a thousand years of peace between them. This is a bigger picture than can be conveyed by speaking of two, so-called, "world wars" of the 20th century. To miss this overview is to fail to understand the message of the Bible prophecy. It is our premise that there are *two world wars* described in the Bible. These two wars are separated by 1,000 years of divinely mandated peace on earth. Understanding this should make end-time prophecy much easier to understand.

Under Observation

For I think that God hath set forth us the apostles last, as it were appointed to death: for we are made a spectacle [theater or drama] unto the world, and to angels, and to men (1 Cor. 4:9).

And having spoiled principalities and powers, he made a shew of them openly, triumphing over them in it (Col. 2:15).

Please bear with me if I seem to be repeating my theme, for I am doing it deliberately. I am strongly convicted that I must make you understand the magnificent revelation in this chapter.

THE BIBLE DESCRIBES TWO WORLD WARS

The first world war did not begin in 1914 nor did it end in 1918. The encyclopedia tells us:

> The assassination of the Austrian archduke Franz Ferdinand in Sarajevo in 1914 proved to be the spark that ignited World War I (1914–18). Called "the Great War," it quickly came to involve all the great powers of Europe and eventually most countries of the world, and cost the lives of more than 8 million soldiers.[3]

That was a major conflict, but it was not the first world war. It was only a part of the first world war.

THE SECOND WORLD WAR DID NOT BEGIN IN 1939

Grolier's Encyclopedia says, "World War II commenced as a localized conflict in eastern Europe and expanded until it merged with a confrontation in the Far East to form a global war of immense proportions. The war began in Europe on September 1, 1939, when Germany attacked Poland."[4]

This recent war brought on the Holocaust which snuffed out the lives of six million Jewish people, among them one and a half million children. Altogether, 52 million people were sacrificed on Moloch's burning altar as a result of the struggle.

The second world war did not end on September 2, 1945, with the formal surrender of Japan, aboard the U.S. battleship *Missouri*, in Tokyo Bay. I now make use of emphasized type and italics. I want these words to shout at you:

The *first world war* began with the fall of Adam and concludes at the Battle of Armageddon. It *includes* the two great conflicts that journalists and historians *call* the First and Second World Wars.

Then comes the *Millennium*.

After the Millennium comes the *second world war*, called the Battle of Gog and Magog. It is a world war and, apparently, is of short duration.[5]

Two World Wars

Let me briefly review a third time the concept that Bible prophecy reveals two world wars. World war one began with the fall of Adam, and it ends at Armageddon when Christ returns and defeats the Antichrist.

Then comes the 1,000-year visible Kingdom — the Millennium. The second world war will be at the end of the Millennium when Satan is loosed for a season.

Prophecy begins on the first pages of your Bible. Here, in Genesis chapter 3 we find both the declaration and outcome of the first world war. This passage is called the protoevangelium, the first declaration of good news to a fallen race of mankind:

> And the LORD God said unto the serpent [Satan][6] Because thou hast done this, thou art cursed above all cattle, and above every beast of the field; upon thy belly shalt thou go, and dust shalt thou eat all the days of thy life: And I will put enmity between thee and the woman, and between thy seed and her seed; it shall bruise thy head, and thou shalt bruise his heel (Gen. 3:14–15).

Planet Earth's world war one is not over yet. We are in the midst of it.

The Outcome of the War Is Already Determined

We are not losing the battle, for Jesus Christ is the captain of our salvation (Heb. 2:10) and the winner of the end-time conflict (Rev. 19:11–21).

Jesus took the disciples to a place called Caesarea

Philippi, at the foot of old Mount Hermon. Here the evil gods Baal and Moloch demanded human sacrifices, and were worshiped. Human sacrifices were offered up to the pagan god Pan during the early Greek period. In Jesus' day, a temple of Caesar Augustus deified that Roman ruler. And yet it was at Caesarea Philippi that Jesus made a most sublime statement, a declaration of victory.

Here Jesus announced the ultimate victory of His Church.

> When Jesus came into the coasts of Caesarea Philippi, he asked his disciples, saying, Whom do men say that I the Son of man am? And they said, Some say that thou art John the Baptist: some, Elias; and others, Jeremias, or one of the prophets. He saith unto them, But whom say ye that I am? And Simon Peter answered and said, Thou art the Christ, the Son of the living God. And Jesus answered and said unto him, Blessed art thou, Simon Barjona: for flesh and blood hath not revealed it unto thee, but my Father which is in heaven. And I say also unto thee, That thou art Peter, and upon this rock I will build my church; and the gates of hell shall not prevail against it. And I will give unto thee the keys of the kingdom of heaven: and whatsoever thou shalt bind on earth shall be bound in heaven: and whatsoever thou shalt loose on earth shall be loosed in heaven (Matt. 16:13–19).[7]

GOD'S PURPOSE REVEALED

Whenever God speaks of His foreordained purposes we had better pay attention. God says Jesus came to destroy Satan's works:

> He that committeth sin is of the devil; for the devil sinneth from the beginning. For this purpose the Son of God was manifested, that he might *destroy the works of the devil* (1 John 3:8, emphasis added).

This was accomplished through Jesus' identification with fallen humanity, culminating with His atoning death on the cross of Calvary (Heb. 2:14–16). Jesus' victory was openly manifested in His resurrection from the dead.

> But now is Christ risen from the dead, and become the firstfruits of them that slept. For since by man came death, by man came also the resurrection of the dead. For as in Adam all die, even so in Christ shall all be made alive. But every man in his own order: Christ the firstfruits; afterward they that are Christ's at his coming. Then cometh the end, when he shall have delivered up the kingdom to God, even the Father; when he shall have put down all rule and all authority and power. For he must reign, till he hath put all enemies under his feet. The last enemy that shall be destroyed is death (1 Cor. 15:20–26).

OUR WARFARE IS SPIRITUAL IN NATURE

> For though we walk in the flesh, we do not war after the flesh: (For the weapons of our warfare are not carnal, but mighty through God to the pulling down of strong holds;) Casting down imaginations [Greek: reasonings], and every high thing that exalteth itself against the knowledge of God, and bringing into captivity every thought to the obedience of Christ (2 Cor. 10:3–5).

> For we wrestle not against flesh and blood,
> but against principalities, against powers, against
> the rulers of the darkness of this world, against
> spiritual wickedness [Greek: wicked spirits] in
> high [Greek: heavenly] places (Eph. 6:12).

RAPTURE AND THE TRIBULATION

The rapture of the church is a victory in the war. Far from being an escapist message, the rapture is a proclamation of the coming victory over Satan and death. It is *by force* that God resurrects those who have died in the faith and removes the church from earth before the tribulation. "Then we which are alive and remain shall be caught up together with them in the clouds, to meet the Lord in the air: and so shall we ever be with the Lord" (1 Thess. 4:17).

The words "caught up" do not give the full meaning of the Greek "*harpazo.*" Strong's Greek gives the meaning, catch up, take by *force*; to seize, carry off by *force*; to seize on, claim for one's self eagerly; to snatch out or away.[8]

After the rapture, the earth is rocked with judgment after judgment (Rev. 6–16). This is the time of the fulfillment of Daniel's 70th week of seven years. The last 3.5 years are called "great tribulation" (Matt. 24:21; Rev. 2:22, 7:14).

Through the witness of the 144,000 (literal) saved and sealed Israelite servants of God (Rev. 7) multitudes are comforted in the tribulation. Many are martyred by the wicked beast, the Antichrist.[9]

The Millennium will not be not brought about through human effort. As my college professor and mentor Dr. Stanley Horton often says, the kingdom of God does not come by the efforts of mankind to bring peace. Rather we see that the Kingdom comes on the heels of earth's greatest tribulation and the outpouring of the judgment of God on this rebellious world. Jesus Christ will establish the thousand year Kingdom at the time of His second coming."[10]

THE LAST WAR

THE END OF THE FIRST WORLD WAR

The first world war ends with the battle of Armageddon at the time of Christ's return with the glorified, raptured church.

> And I saw three unclean spirits like frogs come out of the mouth of the dragon, and out of the mouth of the beast, and out of the mouth of the false prophet. For they are the spirits of devils, working miracles, which go forth unto the kings of the earth and of the whole world, to gather them to the battle of that great day of God Almighty. Behold, I come as a thief. Blessed is he that watcheth, and keepeth his garments, lest he walk naked, and they see his shame. And he gathered them together into a place called in the Hebrew tongue *Armageddon*" (Rev. 16:13–16, emphasis added).

LAST CAMPAIGN OF WORLD WAR I: TARGET — ISRAEL

Note in the following three translations of Zechariah 12:3 that all nations send armies to conquer Jerusalem:

> And in that day will I make Jerusalem a burdensome stone for all people: all that burden themselves with it shall be cut in pieces, though all the people [Greek *gowy* {go'-ee}: nations] of the earth be gathered together against it (Zech. 12:3;KJV).

> On that day I will make Jerusalem a heavy stone for all the peoples; all who lift it shall grievously hurt themselves. And all the *nations* of the earth shall come together against it (Zech. 12:3;NIV).

> On that day, when all the nations of the earth are gathered against her, I will make Jerusalem an

immovable rock for all the *nations*. All who try to move it will injure themselves (Zech. 12:3;NRSV).

JESUS RETURNS WITH THE GLORIFIED CHURCH — ONLY THE JEWS STAND WITH GOD AGAINST ANTICHRIST

Behold, the day of the LORD cometh, and thy spoil shall be divided in the midst of thee. *For I will gather all nations against Jerusalem to battle;* and the city shall be taken, and the houses rifled, and the women ravished; and half of the city shall go forth into captivity, and the residue of the people shall not be cut off from the city. Then shall the LORD go forth, and fight against those nations, as when he fought in the day of battle.

And his feet shall stand in that day upon the mount of Olives, which is before Jerusalem on the east, and the mount of Olives shall cleave in the midst thereof toward the east and toward the west. . . . And the LORD shall be king over all the earth: in that day shall there be one LORD, and his name one. . . .

And Judah also shall fight [Heb. *lacham* — make war] at Jerusalem; and the wealth of all the heathen round about shall be gathered together, gold, and silver, and apparel, in great abundance. . . .

And it shall come to pass, that every one that is left of all the nations which came against Jerusalem shall even go up from year to year to worship the King, the LORD of hosts, and to keep the feast of tabernacles (Zech. 14:1–16, italics added).

THE SHOUT OF VICTORY

In the Book of Revelation, chapter 19, we see a wondrous scene:

And I heard as it were the voice of a great multitude, and as the voice of many waters, and as the voice of mighty thunderings, saying, Alleluia: for the Lord God omnipotent reigneth. Let us be glad and rejoice, and give honour to him: for the marriage of the Lamb is come, and his wife hath made herself ready.

And to her was granted that she should be arrayed in fine linen, clean and white: for the fine linen is the righteousness of saints (Rev. 19:6–8).

And I fell at his feet to worship him. And he said unto me, See thou do it not: I am thy fellowservant, and of thy brethren that have the testimony of Jesus: worship God: for the testimony of Jesus is the spirit of prophecy. And I saw heaven opened, and behold a white horse; and he that sat upon him was called Faithful and True, and in righteousness he doth judge and make war. His eyes were as a flame of fire, and on his head were many crowns; and he had a name written, that no man knew, but he himself. And he was clothed with a vesture dipped in blood: and his name is called The Word of God. And the armies which were in heaven followed him upon white horses, clothed in fine linen, white and clean. And out of his mouth goeth a sharp sword, that with it he should smite the nations: and he shall rule them with a rod of iron: and he treadeth the winepress of the fierceness and wrath of Almighty God. And he hath on his vesture and on his thigh a name written, KING OF KINGS, AND LORD OF LORDS. And I saw an angel standing in the sun; and he cried with a loud voice, saying to all the fowls that fly in the midst of heaven, Come and gather yourselves together unto the supper of the great God; That ye may eat the flesh of kings, and the flesh of captains, and the flesh of mighty men, and the flesh of horses, and of them that sit on them, and the flesh of all men, both free and bond, both small and great. And I saw the beast, and the kings of the earth, and their armies, gathered together to make war against him that sat on the horse, and against his army. And the beast was taken, and with him the false prophet that wrought miracles before him, with which he deceived them that had received the mark of the beast, and them that worshipped his image. These both were cast alive into a lake of fire burning with brimstone. And the remnant were slain with the sword of him that sat upon the horse, which sword proceeded out of his mouth: and all the fowls were filled with their flesh (Rev. 19:10–21).

Thus concludes the first world war.

ONE THOUSAND YEARS OF PEACE

In Revelation 20 we view the binding of Satan for a thousand years. The earth will know a thousand years of true peace. This is the "Regnum Millennium."[11]

> And I saw an angel come down from heaven, having the key of the bottomless pit and a great chain in his hand. And he laid hold on the dragon, that old serpent, which is the Devil, and Satan, and bound him a thousand years, And cast him into the bottomless pit, and shut him up, and set a seal upon him, that he should deceive the nations no more, till the thousand years should be fulfilled: and after that he must be loosed a little season (Rev. 20:1–3).

THE SECOND WORLD WAR FINAL VICTORY

When the devil is released at the end of the Millennium he makes war against God one final time. *This con-*

flict is the second world war. The second world war begins when Satan is released from the pit or abyss, after having been bound and imprisoned there during the one thousand years. At the end of the Millennium, Satan is loosed for a little season, deceives the nations one final time, and heads up the second world war — Gog and Magog. He is defeated and cast into hell forever. The wars are over, never to be known any more for all eternity.

That war is described, briefly, in Revelation 20:

> And when the thousand years are expired, Satan shall be loosed out of his prison, And shall go out to deceive the nations which are in the four quarters of the earth, Gog and Magog, to gather them together to battle: the number of whom is as the sand of the sea. And they went up on the breadth of the earth, and compassed the camp of the saints about, and the beloved city: and fire came down from God out of heaven, and devoured them. And the devil that deceived them was cast into the lake of fire and brimstone, where the beast and the false prophet are, and shall be tormented day and night for ever and ever (Rev. 20:7–10).

Revelation 21 is God's portrait of the eternal state. We will be free from war at last — forever!

> And I saw a new heaven and a new earth: for the first heaven and the first earth were passed away; and there was no more sea. And I John saw the holy city, new Jerusalem, coming down from God out of heaven, prepared as a bride adorned for her husband. And I heard a great voice out of heaven saying, Behold, the tabernacle of God is with men, and he will dwell

with them, and they shall be his people, and God himself shall be with them, and be their God. And God shall wipe away all tears from their eyes; and there shall be no more death, neither sorrow, nor crying, neither shall there be any more pain: for the former things are passed away. And he that sat upon the throne said, Behold, I make all things new. And he said unto me, Write: for these words are true and faithful (Rev. 21:1–5).

Dear friends, the long war is almost over. The final victory is worth any sacrifice in the now season. We have read the last page of the grand old, yet ever new book, the Bible. And there we find out that we are going to win!

> Let's go forward for God
> And resist the foe
> Don't give in to the man of sin
> Our God is mighty
> And we're bound to win
> Satan has an evil force
> To fight against the Lord
> So put on your armor
> Take up your sword
> We're going in the name of the Lord!
> — Neil Moore

Isaiah gives a vivid description of the millennial age in chapters 2 and 11 of the book that bears his name.

And he shall judge among the nations, and shall rebuke many people: and they shall beat their swords into plowshares, and their spears into pruninghooks: nation shall not lift up sword against nation, neither shall they learn war any more (Isa. 2:4).

And there shall come forth a rod out of the stem of Jesse, and a Branch shall grow out of his roots: And the spirit of the LORD shall rest upon him, the spirit of wisdom and understanding, the spirit of counsel and might, the spirit of knowledge and of the fear of the LORD; And shall make him of quick understanding in the fear of the LORD: and he shall not judge after the sight of his eyes, neither reprove after the hearing of his ears: But with righteousness shall he judge the poor, and reprove with equity for the meek of the earth: and he shall smite the earth with the rod of his mouth, and with the breath of his lips shall he slay the wicked. And righteousness shall be the girdle of his loins, and faithfulness the girdle of his reins. The wolf also shall dwell with the lamb, and the leopard shall lie down with the kid; and the calf and the young lion and the fatling together; and a little child shall lead them. And the cow and the bear shall feed; their young ones shall lie down together: and the lion shall eat straw like the ox. And the sucking child shall play on the hole of the asp, and the weaned child shall put his hand on the cockatrice' den. They shall not hurt nor destroy in all my holy mountain: for the earth shall be full of the knowledge of the LORD, as the waters cover the sea.

And in that day there shall be a root of Jesse, which shall stand for an ensign of the people; to it shall the Gentiles seek: and his rest shall be glorious (Isa. 11:1–10).

And God shall wipe away all tears from their eyes; and there shall be no more death, neither sorrow, nor crying, neither shall there be any more pain: for the former things are passed away. And he that sat upon the throne said, Behold, I make all things new. And he said unto me, Write: for these words are true and faithful (Rev. 21:4 –5).

The Prince of Peace is coming. He will end all wars.

NOTES

1 Charles Neider, editor, *The Complete Essays of Mark Twain* (Garden City, NY: Doubleday, 1963), p. 249.

2 See David Lewis's *New 95 Thesis* (Springfield, MO: Menorah Press, 1995).

3 Grolier Electronic Encyclopedia. 1995.

4 Ibid.

5 This is in Revelation 20:8 — not to be confused with the battle of Gog and Magog in Ezekiel chapters 38 and 39.

6 Revelation 12:9.

7 I hope you will study this idea very carefully. You may wish to order a copy of my book *Smashing the Gates of Hell* (Geen Forest, AR: New Leaf Press, 1991), or you can order a 4-page pamphlet *Holy Spirit World Liberation* (free, postpaid).

8 James Strong, *Strong's Exhaustive Concordance of the Bible* (Nashville, TN: Royal Publishers, Inc.).

9 Dwight J. Pentecost, *Things to Come* (Grand Rapids, MI: Zondervan Publishing House, 1958).

10 From a message given by Dr. Horton at the Springfield Regional Eschatology Club.

11 *Regnum:* Latin — kingdom. The word "millennium" is derived from two Latin words: *mille* (1,000) and *annum* (years). Therefore, every time you read "one thousand years" in the Book of Revelation *you are reading Millennium!*

INDEX